THE TRAP

JAMES GOLDSMITH

THE TRAP

M

MACMILLAN

LONDON

First published in France in 1993 by Editions Fixot, Paris
© Editions Fixot, Paris, 1993

This edition first published in Great Britain 1994 by Macmillan Limited
an imprint of Macmillan General Books
Cavaye Place London SW10 9PG
and Basingstoke

Associated companies throughout the world

ISBN 0 333 64224 4

579864 ·

A CIP catalogue record for this book is available from
the British Library

Typeset by CentraCet Limited, Cambridge
Printed by Mackays of Chatham PLC, Chatham, Kent

CONTENTS

Acknowledgements

My thanks for their advice, research and help to Jeffrey Berman, Stewart Boyle, Jacques Broyelle, Jon Cracknell, Michael Crawford, Stephen Dealler, Bruno Erhard-Steiner, Charles Filmer, John Gray, Nicholas Hildyard, Allegra Huston, Robin Jenkins, Richard Lacey, Amory Lovins, Claude Henry Leconte, Jean Moffat, Jeremy Rifkin, Loretta Roccanova, Mycle Schneider, James Thrower, Claire Trocmé, Lori Wallach, Karen West and Bridget Woodman.

James Goldsmith

Preface by Yves Messarovitch

In October 1992, I heard James Goldsmith deliver a lecture in the Grand Amphitheatre of the Sorbonne University in Paris. His audience of over 2,000 people consisted principally of European post-graduate students. That is when I decided that this book should be written. I saw my role not as a sparring partner in a debate but rather as a catalyst. I thought that it might be useful that the ideas expressed by Goldsmith at the Sorbonne be recorded.

1

Measuring or Understanding?

You are clearly troubled by the dilemmas facing modern society.

Every society in the modern world is confronting serious problems which have no simple, universal solutions. But many of the problems have a common root. Science, technology and the economy have been treated by modern societies as ends in themselves, rather than as important tools to enhance well-being. The increase in scientific knowledge, the development of new technologies and economic growth are pursued as if they – and not well-being – should be the objectives of human effort. Social stability and sometimes entire cultures are sacrificed in the pursuit of these goals. I believe that this inversion of values is the cause of many of our ills.

You agree that economic growth and prosperity are useful, although you question their impact on society?

Of course industrial societies, such as our own, need economic prosperity. But I do not accept that economic growth is the principal measure of the success of nations. Look at the US and Great Britain. Modern America has created the greatest economic growth and the greatest material prosperity known to history. During the past fifty years its Gross National Product (GNP) has more than quadrupled, adjusted for inflation.[1] Yet American society is in serious social crisis.

In Great Britain there has also been a surge of material prosperity during the past fifty years. Its GNP has more than trebled in real terms.[2] So according to modern criteria, both these nations have succeeded beyond their grandest dreams. Nonetheless, both nations are profoundly troubled.

What do you believe to be the causes?

One of the defects of modern culture is that we are taught to believe that every problem can be measured in economic terms. But when society's principal tool is measurement rather than understanding, great mistakes follow.

Gross National Product is the official index used to assess prosperity. But GNP measures only activity. It measures neither prosperity nor well-being. For example, if a calamity occurs, such as a hurricane or an earthquake, the immediate consequence is a growth in GNP because activity is increased so as to repair the damage. If a great epidemic hits a community, GNP grows as a result of the construction of new hospitals and the employment of public health workers. If the crime rate increases, GNP grows as more police join the force and new prisons are built. We can take this even further. The cost of cancer in America is estimated at 110 billion dollars per annum,[3] equal to 1.7 per cent of the GNP; the cost of drug abuse is 200 billion dollars,[4] or 3.1 per cent of the GNP; the cost of crime is 163 billion dollars,[5] or 2.6 per cent of the GNP. These three areas alone contribute 473 billion dollars, 7.4 per cent, to the nation's GNP, and they are all growing. These are extreme examples, certainly, but they demonstrate that GNP is not a qualitative measurement but only a measure of activity, good and bad. Nevertheless, all our official statistics are based on the one objective: growth of GNP. And our plans for social development are subservient to it.

What other kinds of false conclusions result from relying on the arithmetic of GNP?

The number is infinite. Take the example of two neighbouring families. In both cases, the mother of the family has decided to spend her days looking after her children and her home. Suddenly, one changes her mind and goes out to get a job. To look after her children, she employs her neighbour. Prior to this change neither of the women contributed to GNP because only activity resulting in monetary exchange is taken into account. While these two women looked after their own families without pay they did not contribute to the official economy and therefore, to the GNP. As soon as they changed their lifestyles and started to receive salaries they immediately contributed to the GNP.

Let's take another example. If a farmer cultivates a variety of crops so as to feed his family, his work is not taken into account in the GNP because the food that he produces is not sold. No monetary transaction has taken place. But if he stops growing a variety of crops and decides to concentrate on only one, a monoculture, then everything changes. He starts to sell his product in the marketplace and in order to feed his family he buys food grown by other farmers. By buying and selling he has become part of the official economy. Indeed, the value of the food he has grown might be counted more than once in GNP depending on how many middlemen have bought and sold it before it reaches the consumer.

GNP only measures activities in the formal economy which give rise to a monetary transaction. Therefore, economic growth can be increased by simply monetizing the informal economy and absorbing it into the official economy. That means destroying the informal economy because it removes it from the traditional framework in which it is embedded, thereby disrupting and destabilizing family relationships and local communities.

We measure the success of nations on the basis of their GNP. That is why we reach false conclusions and make mistakes with tragic consequences. We believe that it is our moral duty to spread to other communities throughout the world the model of society which provides the fastest GNP growth. The fact that growth is achieved at the cost of social stability is ignored. That is how the West has destabilized the world. We have convinced ourselves that there exists only one valid economic and social model: our own. By attempting to impose it universally, we have exported to almost every corner of the world our diseases: crime, drugs, alcoholism, family breakdown, civil disorder in urban slums, accelerated abuse of the environment and all the other problems that we experience daily. We have become so accustomed to these diseases that we explain them away by suggesting that they are no more than the normal phenomena inevitably associated with healthy economic development and progress.

What is more, as we fail to understand the causes

of our problems, we are incapable of solving them. We deal exclusively with the symptoms.

But nonetheless, you agree that economic growth is necessary?

Of course, but it is important to remember that economic growth is only beneficial insofar as it serves the needs of society, consolidating stability and increasing contentment. The economy is a tool to serve us. It is not a demi-god to be served by society. During our conversations, I plan to describe three specific examples of how we have profoundly destroyed our social stability by using ill-conceived modern economic tools.

What are they?

Global free trade, intensive agriculture and nuclear energy. All are pure products of the Enlightenment, and as such are venerated by modern conventional wisdom.

Do you know of any national leaders who understand these problems?

They are rare. Almost every national government has fallen into the trap of counting and measuring

without attempting to understand the consequences. In France over the past twenty years GNP
has grown by 80 per cent,[6] a spectacular performance. And yet during this same period unemployment has grown from 420,000 people to 5.1
million (the official figure is 3.3 million, but the
government's own statistics show that various categories consisting of 1.8 million people have been
omitted).[7] The fact that such growth can be
achieved while at the same time excluding over 5
million people from active participation in society
– a proportion equivalent to over 22 million people
in the USA – should incite a government to
reconsider its policies. Alas, that does not happen.
All we hear is that if we could only achieve one-
half a per cent or 1 per cent faster growth in GNP
all would be saved. In the United Kingdom, despite
growth in GNP of 97 per cent, between 1961 and
1991 the number of those living in poverty grew
from 5.3 million to 11.4 million.[8]

However, every now and then in some unlikely
place, one does come across different thinking. I
once visited the small island of Anguilla in the
West Indies, which at the time had a population of
about 9,000 people. I lunched with the then Prime
Minister. The island is very beautiful. It has long
white beaches and hospitable people. I asked him
about his plans for developing the island. This is

more or less what he answered: 'This island is our island, and we are very happy living here. We have two alternatives. Either we can develop at a reasonable pace and in a way which supplies good jobs and well-being to our people, or we can choose the policy which has been applied in practically all our neighbouring islands. We can aim at rapid and maximum development. After a great deal of thought, we chose the former of these two policies. If we had decided to develop tourism as fast as possible and build great hotels and apartment complexes one next to the other, then we would need to move to a policy of massive immigration so as to be able to operate such an economy. We realized that the inevitable result would be that we would become a minority in our own country. And we would not be spared the growth in crime and drugs and other social tragedies which seem to be the inseparable companions of rapid development, tourism and substantial immigration. Our island would no longer be the same. That is why I have always campaigned that we should be content with optimum development, capable of producing good employment for our people, while at the same time maintaining our way of life.'

Of course, this man had political opponents who held the opposite point of view. In neighbouring islands the price of development land was soaring.

Not too long ago, I visited Vietnam and was able to meet the group of people responsible for trying to find the right strategy for their nation as it emerges from communism. The kind of society which they are aiming at, and which is not yet totally defined, is known as 'the school of thought of Ho Chi Minh'. During our conversations, one question kept returning: How do we move from Marxism-Leninism to the school of thought of Ho Chi Minh without creating more Bangkoks, Rio de Janeiros or Mexico Cities? How do we avoid slums like Harlem and Watts? They had the wisdom to identify one of the major problems of economic development.

One final example. While I was visiting the kingdom of Bhutan in the Himalayas, the King in his annual address to his people declared that he was more interested in Gross National Contentment than in Gross National Product.[9]

So, where do we go from here?

The problems are too complex and too widespread to be answerable with simple solutions. But we can discuss a number of examples which demonstrate how we in the West have lost our way. I hope that in the course of these discussions we might touch on some of the reasons why.

2

The New Utopia: GATT and Global Free Trade

You are opposed to global free trade and therefore to GATT. Why?

Global free trade has become a sacred principle of modern economic theory, a sort of generally accepted moral dogma. That is why it is so difficult to persuade politicians and economists to reassess its effects on a world economy which is changing radically.

The ultimate objective of global free trade is to create a worldwide market in products, services, capital and labour. Its instrument to achieve this is GATT, the General Agreement on Tariffs and Trade.

I believe that GATT and the theories on which it is based are flawed. If it is implemented, it will impoverish and destabilize the industrialized world while at the same time cruelly ravaging the third world.

Remind us of the economic theory on which GATT is based.

The principal theoretician of free trade was David Ricardo, a British economist of the early nineteenth century.[1] He believed in two interrelated concepts: specialization and comparative advantage. According to Ricardo, each nation should specialize in those activities in which it excels, so that it can have the greatest advantage relative to other countries. Thus, a nation should narrow its focus of activity, abandoning certain industries and developing those in which it has the largest comparative advantage. As a result, international trade would grow as nations export their surpluses and import the products that they no longer manufacture, efficiency and productivity would increase in line with economies of scale and prosperity would be enhanced. But these ideas are not valid in today's world.

Why?

During the past few years, 4 billion people have suddenly entered the world economy. They include the populations of China, India, Vietnam, Bangladesh, and the countries that were part of the Soviet empire, among others. These populations are growing fast; in thirty-five years, that 4 billion is forecast to expand to over 6.5 billion.[2] These nations have very high levels of unemployment and those people who do find jobs offer their labour for a tiny fraction of the pay earned by workers in the developed world. For example, forty-seven Vietnamese or forty-seven Filipinos can be employed for the cost of one person in a developed country, such as France.[3]

Until recently, these 4 billion people were separated from our economy by their political systems, primarily communist or socialist, and because of a lack of technology and of capital. Today all that has changed. Their political systems have been transformed, technology can be transferred instantaneously anywhere in the world on a microchip, and capital is free to be invested wherever the anticipated yields are highest.

The principle of global free trade is that anything can be manufactured anywhere in the world to be sold anywhere else. That means that these new entrants into the world economy are in direct competition with the workforces of developed countries. They have become part of the same global labour market. Our economies, therefore, will be subjected to a completely new type of competition. For example, take two enterprises, one in the developed world and one in Vietnam. Both make an identical product destined to be sold in the same market, say the USA, Great Britain or France; both can use identical technology; both have access to the same pool of international capital. The only difference is that the Vietnamese enterprise can employ forty-seven people where the French enterprise can employ only one. You don't have to be a genius to understand who will be the winner in such a contest.

In most developed nations, the cost to an average manufacturing company of paying its workforce is an amount equal to between 25 per cent and 30 per cent of sales. If such a company decides to maintain in its home country only its head office and sales force, while transferring its production to a low-cost area, it will save about 20 per cent of sales volume. Thus, a company with sales of 500 million dollars will increase its pre-tax profits by up to 100 million dollars every year. If, on the other hand, it decides to maintain its production at home, the enterprise will be unable to compete with low-cost imports and will perish.

It must surely be a mistake to adopt an economic policy which makes you rich if you eliminate your national workforce and transfer production abroad, and which bankrupts you if you continue to employ your own people.

But the companies that move offshore are those which employ large labour forces. Surely the new jobs that will be created by the high-tech industries of the future will compensate.

High-tech industries can, indeed, survive and prosper under these circumstances, for the very reason that they are highly automated and therefore employ few people. Labour is no more than a minor item in the overall cost of the products they make. But obviously they cannot compensate for the lost manufacturing jobs: the fact that they employ few people means that they are incapable of employing very many. As soon as they need to employ a reasonable number, they will be forced to move offshore. For example, IBM is moving its disk-drive business from America and Western Europe to low labour-cost countries. According to the *Wall Street Journal*: 'IBM plans to establish this new site as a joint venture with an undetermined Asian partner and use non-IBM employees so that it will be easier . . . to move to an even lower-cost region when warranted . . . Moving from higher-cost regions to Asia cuts in half the cost of assembling a disk drive.' Mr Zschau of IBM 'admitted that the moves will put IBM on only even footing with its competitors'.[4] The aircraft manufacturer Boeing has announced that it will transfer some of its production to China.[5] The sort of companies that created Silicon Valley, like Hewlett-Packard and Advanced Micro Devices, are also shifting employment to low-wage countries.[6]

Proponents of global free trade constantly say that exporting such high-tech products as very fast trains, airplanes and satellites will create jobs on a large scale. Alas, this is not true. The recent 2.1 billion dollar contract selling very fast French trains to South Korea has resulted in the maintenance, for four years, of only 800 jobs in France: 525 for the main supplier and 275 for the subcontractors.[7] Much of the work is carried out in Korea by Asian companies using Asian labour. What is more, following the transfer of technology to South Korea, in a few years' time Asia will be able to buy very fast trains directly from South Korea and bypass France. As for planes and satellites, the numbers employed in these industries in France have fallen steadily. Over the five years from 1987 to 1992, they have declined from 123,000 to 111,000 and are forecast to fall to 102,000 in the short term.[8]

One of the big mistakes that we make is that when we talk about balancing trade we think exclusively in monetary terms. If we export one billion dollars' worth of goods and import products of the same value, we conclude that our overseas trade is in balance. The value of our exports is equal to that of our imports. But this is a superficial analysis and leads to wrong conclusions. The products that we export must necessarily be those which use only a small amount of labour. If not, they would be unable to compete with products manufactured in low labour-cost countries and so would be unexportable. The number of people employed annually to produce one billion dollars' worth of high-tech products in the developed nations could be under a thousand. But the number of people employed in the low-cost areas to manufacture the goods that we import would be in the tens of thousands, because these are not high-tech products but ones produced with traditional levels of employment. So, our trade might be in balance in monetary terms, but if we look beyond the monetary figures we find that there is a terrible imbalance in terms of employment. That is how we export jobs and import unemployment.

But many economists believe that the growth in service industries will compensate for lost jobs in manufacturing.

Even service industries will be subjected to substantial transfers of employment to low-cost areas. Today, through satellites, you can remain in constant contact with offices in distant lands. This means that companies employing large back offices can close them and shift employment to any other part of the world. Swissair has recently transferred a significant part of its accounts department to India.

Still, certain services cannot be transferred overseas, such as health and education.

Indeed, but let's think that through to its practical conclusion. A nation's economy is split into two broad segments, one which produces wealth and the other which dispenses it. That in no way means that the latter is inferior; it includes such vital activities as health and education. Despite the fact that both kinds of activities are measured by GNP, one cannot reduce that part of our economy which produces wealth and expect to be able to maintain the other part which dispenses it. You must earn what you spend.

Presumably, the exchange rates between various currencies also have a substantial impact on the power to compete.

Of course. When Ricardo calculated comparative advantage, he did so in money terms. If a product costs X French francs in France and Y US dollars in America, all you need to do is to convert dollars into francs at the going rate of exchange and it will be clear where the advantage lies. In other words, the nation in which the product is cheaper is the nation that has the comparative advantage.

But this calculation can be brutally and suddenly transformed by a devaluation or a revaluation of one of the currencies. In 1981, one dollar was worth 4.25 French francs; by 1985, the dollar had risen sharply and was worth 10 French francs; by 1992, it had fallen again and was worth only 4.80 French francs. So take a product which in 1981 had the same cost whether manufactured in America or in France. Four years later, in 1985, it became more than twice as expensive in America as in France. This was no more than a reflection of the increased value of the dollar relative to the franc. Yet, according to Ricardo, each nation is supposed to specialize in those products in which it has a comparative advantage. If you followed this reasoning, industries on which you might have concentrated in America in 1981 would have had to be abandoned in 1985. And the reason would have been that the comparative advantage would have disappeared purely for monetary reasons. Then as the dollar fell again in 1992, the theory would have required that you recreate the industry in the United States. This is obvious nonsense. No one should sacrifice and recreate industries merely to be in rhythm with fluctuations in exchange rates.

Of course, those who believe in global free trade reject your arguments. In the first place, they cite the joint study published by the OECD and the World Bank which states that the application of the GATT proposals would increase world income by 213 billion dollars a year.[9] How can we turn down such growth?

If you study the reports, you will find that the increase is forecast to come about in ten years' time. Yes, 213 billion dollars is a large sum of money, but to assess its significance you must compare it to the world's GNP as it is forecast to be in ten years' time. 213 billion dollars represents no more than 0.7 per cent.[10] What is more, the General Secretary of the OECD described the report as being 'highly theoretical'.

It is also claimed that global free trade means that consumers will benefit from being able to buy cheaper imported products manufactured with low-cost labour.

Consumers are not just people who buy products, they are the same people who earn a living by working, and who pay taxes. As consumers they may be able to buy certain products more cheaply, although when Nike moved its manufacturing from the US to Asia, shoe prices did not drop. Instead profit margins rose. But the real cost to consumers of cheaper goods will be that they will lose their jobs, get paid less for their work and have to face higher taxes to cover the social cost of increased unemployment. Consumers are also citizens, many of whom live in towns. As unemployment rises and poverty increases, towns and cities will grow even more unstable. So the benefits of cheap imported products will be heavily outweighed by the social and economic costs they bring with them.

I understand your argument about increased unemployment, but why should earnings be reduced?

According to figures published by the US Department of Labor,[11] since 1973 real hourly and weekly earnings, in inflation-adjusted dollars, have already dropped respectively by 13.4 per cent and 19.2 per cent, and that was before the most recent GATT negotiations known as the Uruguay Round. If 4 billion people enter the same world market for labour and offer their work at a fraction of the price paid to people in the developed world, it is obvious that such a massive increase in supply will reduce the value of labour. Also, organized labour will lose practically all its negotiating power. When trade unions ask for concessions, the answer will be: If you put too much pressure on us, we will move offshore where we can get much cheaper labour, which does not seek job protection, long holidays, and all the other items that you want to negotiate.

Global free trade will shatter the way in which value-added is shared between capital and labour. Value-added is the increase of value obtained when you convert raw materials into a manufactured product. In mature societies, we have been able to develop a general agreement as to how it should be shared. That agreement has been reached through generations of political debate, elections, strikes, lockouts and other conflicts. Overnight that agreement will be destroyed by the arrival of huge populations willing to undercut radically the salaries earned by our workforces. The social divisions that this will cause will be deeper than anything ever envisaged by Marx.

It is interesting to note that many US economists believe that the inflationary forces which normally follow a period of lax monetary policy will not occur in the same way on this occasion. They believe that the continued lowering of earnings resulting from global free trade, including the first effects of NAFTA (the North American Free Trade Agreement, which created an open market between Mexico, the US and Canada), will restrain inflation despite the fact that the Federal Reserve has maintained a loose monetary policy for one of the longest periods on record. In other words, the workforce will bear the brunt of the consequences of a prolonged policy of easy money by accepting reduced earnings to compensate for its inevitable inflationary effects.

Who will be the losers and who will be the winners under a system of global free trade?

The losers will, of course, be those people who become unemployed as a result of production being moved to low-cost areas. There will also be those who lose their jobs because their employers do not move offshore and are not able to compete with cheap imported products. Finally, there will be those whose earning capacity is reduced following the shift in the sharing of value-added away from labour.

The winners will be those who can benefit from an almost inexhaustible supply of very cheap labour. They will be the companies who move their production offshore to low-cost areas; the companies who can pay lower salaries at home; and those who have capital to invest where labour is cheapest, and who as a result will receive larger dividends. But they will be like the winners of a poker game on the *Titanic*. The wounds inflicted on their societies will be too deep, and brutal consequences could follow.

The new phenomenon of our age is the emergence of transnational corporations, with the ability to move production at will anywhere in the world, in order to systematically benefit from lower wages wherever they are to be found. Transnational corporations now account for one-third of global output; their global annual sales have reached 4.8 trillion dollars, which is greater than total international trade. The largest 100 multinational corporations control about one-third of all foreign direct investment.[12] The globalization of the market is vital to them, both to produce cheaply and to sell universally. Because they do not necessarily owe allegiance to the countries where they operate, there is a divorce between the interests of the transnational corporations and those of society.

You must remember that one of the characteristics of developing countries is that a small handful of people controls the overwhelming majority of the nation's resources. It is these people who own most of their nation's industrial, commercial and financial enterprises and who assemble the cheap labour which is used to manufacture products for the developed world. Thus, it is the poor in the rich countries who will subsidize the rich in the poor countries. This will have a serious impact on the social cohesion of nations.

What are your thoughts about the World Trade Organization?

That is the organization which is supposed to replace GATT, regulate international trade, and lead us to global economic integration. It is yet another international bureaucracy whose function-aries will be largely autonomous. They report to over 120 nations and therefore, in practice, to nobody. Each nation will have one vote out of 120. Thus, America and every European nation will be handing over ultimate control of its economy to an unelected, uncontrolled, group of international bureaucrats.

Don't the developed nations have a moral responsi-bility to open their markets to the third world?

Let me start by quoting from a report by Herman Daly and Robert Goodland, published by the World Bank.

If by wise policy or blind luck, a country has managed to control its population growth, provide social insurance, high wages, reasonable working hours and other benefits to its working class (i.e. most of its citizens), should it allow these benefits to be competed down to the world average by unregulated trade? . . . This levelling of wages will be overwhelmingly downward due to the vast number and rapid growth rate of under-employed populations in the third world. Northern labourers will get poorer, while Southern labourers will stay much the same.[13]

But the application of GATT will also cause a great tragedy in the third world. Modern economists believe that an efficient agriculture is one that produces the maximum amount of food for the minimum cost, using the least number of people. That is bad economics. When you intensify the methods of agriculture and substantially reduce the number of people employed on the land, those who become redundant are forced into the cities. Everywhere you travel in the world you see those terrible slums made up of people who have been uprooted from the land. But, of course, the hurt is deeper. Throughout the third world, families are broken, the countryside is deserted, and social stability is destroyed. This is how the slums in Brazil, known as *favelas*, came into existence.

It is estimated that there are still 3.1 billion people in the world who live from the land. If GATT manages to impose worldwide the sort of productivity achieved by the intensive agriculture of nations such as Australia, then it is easy to calculate that about 2 billion of these people will become redundant. Some of these GATT refugees will move to urban slums. But a large number of them will be forced into mass migration. Today, as we discuss these issues, there is great concern about the 2 million refugees who have been forced to flee the tragic events in Rwanda. GATT, if it 'succeeds', will create mass migrations of refugees on a scale a thousand times greater. We will have profoundly and tragically destabilized the world's population.

But why do third world nations themselves support global free trade?

We must distinguish between the populations on the one hand and their ruling elites on the other. It is the elites who are in favour of global free trade. It is they who will be enriched. In India there have been demonstrations of up to one million people opposing the destruction of their rural communities, their culture and their traditions. In the Philippines several hundred thousand farmers protested against GATT because it would destroy their system of agriculture.

Vandana Shiva is an eminent Indian philosopher and physicist. She is Director of the Research Foundation for Science, Technology and National Resource Policy, and is the Science and Environment Adviser of the Third World Network. In India, she says, global free trade 'will mean a further destruction of our communities, uprooting of millions of small peasants from the land, and their migration into the slums of overcrowded cities. GATT destroys the cultural diversity and social stability of our nation ... GATT, for us, implies recolonization.'[14]

Without global free trade, how could the developing nations emerge?

Those who wish to industrialize should form free trade areas, such as the trading regions currently being created in Latin America and South-East Asia. These areas should consist of nations with economies which are reasonably similar in terms of development and wage structures. Trading regions would enter into mutually beneficial bilateral agreements with other regions in the world. Freedom to transfer technology and capital would be maintained. Thus commercial organizations wishing to sell their products in any particular region would have to produce locally, importing capital and technology, and creating local employment and development. That is the way to create prosperity and stability in the developing world without destroying our own.

Some would say that Europe's employment problem is not GATT, but just the result of the old-fashioned diseases that one finds in uncompetitive, inflexible and spoiled societies. The welfare state is out of control; social costs borne by employers discourage the creation of new jobs; high government expenditure and taxation stifle the economy; state intervention is paralyzing; corporatism blocks remedial action, etc. Is that not true?

It is partially true, and those diseases must be treated forcefully. But even if the treatment is successful, it will not solve the problems created by global free trade. Imagine that we were able to reduce at a stroke social charges and taxation so as to diminish the cost of labour by a full third. All it would mean is that instead of being able to employ forty-seven Vietnamese or forty-seven Filipinos for the price of one Frenchman, you could employ only thirty-one.

In any case, as we have already discussed, you must remember the example of France, where, over the past twenty years, spectacular growth in GNP has been surpassed by an even more spectacular rise in unemployment. This has taken place while Europe has progressively opened its market to international free trade. How can we accept a system which increases unemployment from 420,000 to 5.1 million during a period in which the economy has grown by 80 per cent?

You must understand that we are not talking about normal competition between nations. The 4 billion people who are joining the world economy have been part of a wholly different society, indeed, a different world. It is absurd to believe that suddenly we can create a global free trade area, a common market with, for example, China, without massive changes leading to consequences that we cannot anticipate.

Why is it not possible to repeat our successes in enriching countries like Taiwan, Hong Kong, South Korea and Singapore?

The combined population of those countries is about 75 million people, so the scale of the problem is quite different. The US might be able to achieve a similar success with Mexico and, progressively, Western Europe could accommodate Eastern Europe. But attempting to integrate 4 billion people at once is blind utopianism.

In any case, each of those countries was a beneficiary of the Cold War. During that period, one or other of the superpowers sought to bring every part of the world into its camp. If one failed to fill the void, the other stepped in. That is why very favourable economic treatment was granted by the West to South Korea after the Korean War, and to Taiwan, Singapore and Hong Kong while China was considered a major communist threat.

Special economic concessions combined with their cheap and skilled labour forces made them successful. Over the past thirty years the balance of trade between these countries and the West has resulted in a transfer of tens of billions of dollars from us to them. The West has been haemorrhaging jobs and capital so as to help make them rich.

What do you recommend?

We must start by rejecting the concept of global free trade and we must replace it by regional free trade. That does not mean closing off any region from trading with the rest of the world. It means that each region is free to decide whether or not to enter into bilateral agreements with other regions. We must not simply open our markets to any and every product regardless of whether it benefits our economy, destroys our employment or destabilizes our society.

Does that not mean that we will cut ourselves off from innovation in other parts of the world?

No. Freedom of movement of capital should be maintained. If a Japanese or a European company wishes to sell its products in North America, it should invest in America. It should bring its capital and its technology, build factories in America, employ American people and become a corporate citizen of America. The same is true for American and Japanese firms wishing to sell their products in Europe.

Think about the difference between the GATT proposals and those I have just outlined. GATT makes it almost imperative for enterprises in the developed world to close down their production, eliminate their employees and move their factories to low-cost labour areas. What I am suggesting is the reverse: that to gain access to our markets foreign corporations would have to build factories, employ our people and contribute to our economies. It is the difference between life and death.

But won't that reduce competition?

Competition is an economic tool which is necessary to promote efficiency, to apply downward pressure on prices and to stimulate innovation, diversity and choice. Vigorous competition needs a free market that is large and in which cartels and other limitations on competitive forces are forbidden. Europe and NAFTA are economically the two largest free trade areas ever created in history. Both are more than big enough to ensure highly competitive internal markets. They are vast and open and free and welcoming to innovations from anywhere in the world. Every significant corporation worldwide would have to come and compete, because no corporation could afford to bypass them – their markets are much too big and prosperous. But such competition would be constructive, not destructive.

Many will answer you by saying that you cannot export to other regions if you maintain a regional economy. There would be retaliation.

Take a look at Japan: the Japanese have certainly been able to export over the decades during which they protected their economy. In any case, bilateral trade agreements would allow for the exchange of products in a way which suited all parties. And our corporations would be free to invest and compete throughout the world.

What other recommendations do you have?

I totally reject the concept of specialization. Specializing in certain activities automatically means abandoning others. But one of the most valuable elements of our national patrimony is the existing complex of small and medium-sized businesses and craftsmen covering a wide range of activities. A healthy economy must be built like a pyramid. At the peak are the large corporations. At the base is the diversity of small enterprises. An economy founded on a few specialized corporations can produce large profits, but because the purpose of specialization is to streamline production, it cannot supply the employment which naturally results from a broadly diversified economy. Only a diversified economy is able to supply the jobs which can allow people to participate fully in society.

It is extraordinary to read economists commenting on the state of the nation. They believe that the profits of large corporations and the level of the stock markets are a reliable guide to the health of society and the economy. A healthy economy does not exclude from active participation a substantial proportion of its citizens.

THE TRAP

You face a difficult problem in converting the British to these ideas. Britain has a long tradition of almost unconditional belief in free trade.

The origin of Britain's belief in free trade goes back to the early nineteenth century. It was in Britain, at that time, that the Industrial Revolution was born. The new industrial barons, whose power was growing in step with the expansion of British industry, needed ample and low-cost labour to populate their factories. The idea was that by importing cheap food from the colonies, British farms would be unable to compete. This would result in an exodus of farm workers to the cities. At that time, 80 per cent of the British population lived outside urban areas.[15] Once the farmers who had lost their livelihood reached the towns, they could be employed cheaply because cheap food was available from the colonies. What is more, the money that left Britain to buy the cheap food was recycled back to Britain to buy manufactured goods. At the time, Britain had a quasi-monopoly of manufacturing. Those were the dynamics which led to the repeal of the Corn Laws, which protected British agriculture, in 1846.

Today the circumstances are precisely reversed. Now only 1.1 per cent of the British workforce is employed in agriculture;[16] instead of a need for labour in the towns, there is chronic unemployment; and the money that leaves Britain to pay for imports no longer returns to buy British manufactured products. It goes to Japan or Korea or anywhere else in the world. The result is that Britain has a trade deficit in practically every major category of manufactured goods. And even though some of the large companies make good profits, 25 per cent of all households and nearly one child in three live in poverty.[17]

One of the greatest fallacies in economic thinking is that the funds that flow away from a nation as a result of a negative balance of trade, or of capital outflows, will automatically be recycled. Many economists believe that if, for example, the countries of Asia export more than they import, the excess cash will be invested abroad and ultimately this inflow will equal the outflow suffered by those with a trade deficit. Their assumption appears to be that for strictly mathematical reasons a nation's accounts must balance. But when a foreign nation does direct its excess cash to a nation suffering a deficit, that money usually returns in the form of investments in assets or in fixed interest debt. Those assets thereby become the property of a foreign owner and their earnings flow to that owner. To illustrate the consequences, imagine a game of poker in which you lose more cash than you possess. Instead of paying in cash, you hand over ownership of your house and you continue to live in it as a tenant paying rent. Are we seriously to believe that such a transaction has had a nil effect on your financial position?

The US is now starting to suffer from this very problem. *The Economist* writes: 'Since 1981, America has shifted from being the world's biggest creditor to its biggest debtor, thanks to its persistent current accounts deficits. At the end of 1993, America had net foreign-debt obligations of $556 billion.'[18] And the *Washington Post* in an editorial, explains: 'Now the American economy has begun to pay out more in earnings on foreign investments at home, and on the country's huge accumulation of foreign debt, than it is earning on American investments abroad. It's the cost of running those big trade deficits year after year. They are being financed by foreign capital, and like any debtor country, the United States has to pay for the use of the money . . . Note that the American economy is now borrowing abroad to pay interest on its earlier foreign borrowings. That is no healthier for a country than it is for a business or a household. And how long can it go on? As long as foreigners are willing to lend. If and when their willingness diminishes, you will see it in higher interest rates. Should that happen, Americans would, as the economists say, have to adjust. That, as the Latin American debtor countries can testify, means a lower standard of living. The longer the foreign deficits pile up, the harder that adjustment will be.'[19]

In any case when funds leave a nation, those who receive them are free to invest anywhere in the world. And they will invest wherever the anticipated returns are highest. They will not necessarily choose societies which are bleeding to death.

When a system is valid in one set of circumstances, it is extremely unlikely to be valid in diametrically opposite circumstances. One would hope that this observation alone might prompt the British political elites to reassess their economic doctrine with an open mind.

We seem to have forgotten the purpose of the economy. The present British government is proud of the fact that labour costs less in Britain than in other European countries. But it does not yet understand that in a system of global free trade its competitors will no longer be in Europe but in the low-cost countries. And compared to labour in those countries, Britain's labour will remain uncompetitive no matter how deeply the British government decides to impoverish its people.

In the great days of the USA, Henry Ford stated that he wanted to pay high wages to his employees so that they could become his customers and buy his cars. Today we are proud of the fact that we pay low wages. We have forgotten that the economy is a tool to serve the needs of society, and not the reverse. The ultimate purpose of the economy is to create prosperity with stability.

What do you mean by stability?

Stability does not mean ossification or standing still. A stable society can accommodate necessary change without social breakdown. A stable society can benefit from responsible economic growth without destroying itself.

How would you convince Germany of the merits of regional trade in view of the German elites' commitment to globalism?

The Germans should understand that by far their largest customers are their neighbours; about 70 per cent of Germany's exports are sold within Europe. Germany cannot want to see its principal customers impoverished as a result of haemorrhaging jobs and capital. German prosperity depends on the prosperity of the other nations of Europe;

Germany's social stability will be deeply influenced by that of its neighbours; and, no matter how advanced its industrial skills, Germany will suffer from the transfer of production to low-cost areas, just like the rest of the developed world. What is more, under GATT Germany will have to share its residual markets with imports from Japan, Korea and other countries.

How would you sum up the effects of regional free trade?

Let us imagine that Europe returns to the original concept of the Treaty of Rome, which was the basis for the creation of the European Community. Economically, its purpose was to establish the largest free market in the world. Within Europe, there would be no tariffs, no barriers, and a free and competitive market. Trade with nations outside Europe would be subject to a single tariff. This concept was known as community preference. In other words, priority would be given to European jobs and industry. About twenty years ago, quietly, the technocrats who run Europe started to alter this basic principle and move progressively towards international free trade. Ever since, unemployment in Europe has swollen despite growth in GNP. The Treaty of Maastricht enshrines this change

and makes global free trade one of the fundamental principles on which the new Europe is to
be built.

If we were to return to the ideas of our founding
fathers and reimpose community preference,
overnight all the enterprises which have moved
their production to low-cost countries would have
to return. They could no longer competitively
import products manufactured outside Europe.
Factories would be built, Europeans would be
employed, the economy would prosper and social
stability would return. What is more, international
corporations wishing to sell their products within
Europe would also have to build, employ and
participate in the European economy. From being
a community which, at the moment, reeks of
death, it would all of a sudden become one of the
most exciting places in which to invest and participate. And European corporations would go out to
invest and contribute to the prosperity of regions
throughout the world. The same is true for North
America.

Insofar as free trade areas consisting of developing economies are concerned, they also would
prosper. For example, currently free trade areas
are being formed in Latin America and in South-
East Asia. Most North American, European and
Japanese corporations will wish to sell their

products in these large markets. To do so, they will have to transfer capital and technology, build factories in Latin America and South-East Asia and employ Latin Americans and Asians. By participating in these economies, they would encourage development.

GATT must be rejected. It is too profoundly flawed to be a stepping stone to a better system. The damage it will inflict on the communities of both the developed world and the third world will be intolerable.

3

Nations, Artificial States and Populated Spaces

Currently there are about thirty wars being fought throughout the world. Why do you think that following the end of the Cold War, there has been such a proliferation of conflict?

The causes of most of these conflicts fall into a relatively small number of categories. Many are due not to aggression by a foreign power, but to the desire of real nations to be liberated from the artificial states that have been imposed on them.

Most artificial states have come into existence when the ruling elites of the West redrew the map of the world on false premises. The conventional wisdom, on which they based their action, refused to accept the existence of nationhood and therefore was unable to distinguish between nations, artificial states and populated spaces. During the Cold War, unnatural political structures were held in place by the uneasy world order maintained by the superpowers. Nations now wish to recover their freedom and the result, inevitably, is conflict.

How do you define a nation?

It is a land whose citizens, in their overwhelming majority, share a common culture, sense of identity, heritage and traditional roots.

How would you distinguish a nation from what you describe as an artificial state?

Let me give you a few examples.

The Czechs and the Slovaks are two nations which in 1918 were forced into a single state, Czechoslovakia. As soon as they became free after the fall of the Berlin Wall, they discarded their artificial union and peacefully divorced.

Yugoslavia was an artificial state, also created in 1918, which grouped together Serbs, Croats, Slovenes and other nations into six 'republics' and two 'autonomous regions', all dominated by the power of the Serbs. The present war reflects the desire of these different nations to establish their independence. It is complicated by the territorial urge to obtain as much space as possible.

The artificial state of Belgium was formed in 1831. It attempted to bring together the Walloon and Flemish peoples. After 162 years of conflict, the constitution was altered in 1993 so as to grant greater autonomy to the constituent nations. Many believe that this was only a first step towards effective separation.

Two of these three examples of nations attempting to free themselves from artificial states are being resolved peacefully, Czechoslovakia by negotiated divorce and Belgium by constitutional evolution. The other, Yugoslavia, is condemned to war and ongoing tragedy.

This is a worldwide phenomenon. In the Americas, the most obvious example of a separatist movement is in Canada. In Europe, we have the emerging separatist political party in Italy known as the Lombardy League; as well as various movements, often violent, which seek national reconstruction: the Basque separatists and, further east, the Kurds whose people are divided among a number of countries and seek a homeland of their own.

In the ex-Soviet Union, where nationhood was suppressed, examples abound, typically in Armenia, Georgia, Moldova and Tadjikistan.

Africa is worst of all. The colonial powers inflicted profound damage on that continent, driving frontiers straight through the ancestral territories of nations. For example, we drew a line through Somalia, separating off part of the Somali people and placing them within Kenya. We did the same by splitting the great Masai nation between

Kenya and Tanzania. Elsewhere, of course, we created the usual artificial states. Nigeria consists of four principal nations: the Hausa, Igbo, Yoruba, and Fulani peoples. It has already suffered a terrible war which killed hundreds of thousands of people and which settled nothing. Sudan, Chad, Djibouti, the Senegal, Mali, Burundi and, of course, Rwanda are among the many other states that are riven by conflict.

Our present policy is no better. Even after the fall of the racist apartheid regime, we are unable to understand that South Africa is an artificial state combining a number of proud and great black nations. They were subjugated and held in check by the white colonialist power, but now they seek their autonomy. As ever, the policy of the West remains colonial in spirit, as we refuse to understand that the problems are no longer principally between black and white but are between nations trapped in a straitjacket created by the West. So our leaders work to maintain the imperial structure, by replacing one imperial power with another. They back the Xhosa nation to dominate all others. We are witnessing an attempt to form another Yugoslavia.

As for Somalia, the stated purpose of the recent intervention was to restore hope by delivering food. Then our colonialist impulse returned. We came to believe that we knew how to solve Somalia's problems and we converted 'Operation Restore Hope' into a military expedition to 'Nation Build'. The result, according to the US Ambassador in Somalia, is that 'There is no more Somalia. Somalia's gone. You can call the place where the Somali people live "Somalia", but Somalia as a state disappeared in 1991.'[1] That, of course, was the date of the US-led military invasion which left Somalia in a state of anarchy. It is almost unbelievable that despite the tragedy and chaos we have inflicted on Africa and despite our inability to solve our own problems, we are still arrogant enough to believe that we have the knowledge, indeed the duty, to subjugate other nations and force our ideas upon them.

You do not mean to imply that a nation cannot integrate foreigners?

Of course not. Indeed, nations need new blood and new ideas. But they can only absorb a limited amount at a time. They cannot allow themselves to be overwhelmed by immigration otherwise they will lose their identity and cease to be nations. Newcomers who are welcomed into a nation should want to honour and respect the customs of their new home. They must not step on shore or over the border and reject the national culture. If they do, the inevitable results are hostility, intolerance and conflict.

How does a nation differ from what you describe as a 'populated space'?

Many modern intellectuals have taught that a geographic space, once populated, ipso facto becomes a nation. In other words, they believe that all sorts of peoples, drawn from completely different cultures and ethnic groups, can be gathered together, mixed up and deposited on a given territory and thereby a nation will be created. In reality, this merely populates a space which over a very long period of time might evolve into a nation.

What about religious wars?

The strengthening of Islam is the main factor in the recent increase in religious wars. But that is itself a natural reaction against the excessive intrusion of western modernism.

In Iran, for example, the Shah attempted to westernize his country in one generation. He collectivized the farms, uprooted the rural populations and chased them into towns whose slums expanded massively, undertook an intensive programme of industrialization and, so as to replace the traditional customs, imported western culture. What is more, he challenged the religion of his people. How could a nation fail to reject such all-embracing aggression? Of course, action creates reaction. And when the action is exaggerated the reaction is all the stronger.

Algeria is another nation in deep trouble. Here again, the West sought to impose its culture and replace ancestral traditions by a kind of western progressive socialism, a blend of the ideas much appreciated by fashionable intellectuals. The results were the same as ever: uprooting of the rural population; relatively unsuccessful industrial-ization; mass migration to urban areas leading to the tragic development of slums; an extension of welfare in an attempt to calm a destabilized popu-lation, leading to the emergence of a dependent underclass; population explosion; social break-down; an epidemic of crime; and finally a brutal rejection of the destructive foreign culture that had been forced on the Algerian people.

It is interesting to compare the West's reaction to the expulsion of Jean-Bertrand Aristide follow-ing his democratic election in Haiti, with western attitudes towards Algeria after the election was halted when the Islamic political parties were on the brink of being democratically elected. Insofar as

Haiti is concerned, there has been infinite gesticulation and posturing in front of the TV cameras, military intervention and politicians insisting that the results of democratic elections must be respected universally. Yet virtual silence has greeted the reversal of a democratic election in Algeria. The West cannot understand a democratic rejection of its ideas. For the West such a rejection is a sign of either dementia or evil.

How do you explain this?

The West believes that its destiny is to guide or coerce diverse human cultures into a single global civilization. It cannot tolerate the coexistence in the world of different cultures. The principal reason for this is that the West really is convinced that it has discovered the only model of society which benefits humanity, and therefore that it has a moral duty to ensure that the whole world adopts that model. The debate concerning Haiti is a good illustration. The key advisers to the Clinton administration propose that the right to democracy be universal and that the global community should guarantee this as a legal entitlement. Consequently the US Administration mounted a military intervention in Haiti. As Jeane Kirkpatrick writes: 'If we act against Haiti, we should do so understanding that there are fifty-five countries judged by the Freedom House analysis to be "not free".[2]

This acute form of cultural imperialism is reinforced by international business, which considers that it would benefit from the destruction of social diversity and its replacement by a global monoculture hungry for western-type products.

What is your view of the United States itself? In your view is it a nation, an artificial state or a populated space?

America has changed path several times during its history. From the early eighteenth century, the immigrant population was principally of European cultural traditions. Then occurred the terrible tragedy of the mass importation of slaves.

James Madison, after his retirement from the Presidency, foresaw the social consequences of this change. Even though he himself was a slave owner, he believed in emancipation. But he understood that the slaves had been stripped of their cultures and identities and that they would be excluded from, or would reject, the prevalent white culture. He concluded that it would be almost impossible to heal the social wounds and that many of the black peoples, therefore, would remain separate and alienated, while the white population would retain a sense of guilt. Both ethnic groups would suffer as, of course, would the nation. It is well known that Madison believed that following emancipation liberated slaves should return to Africa and that America should act with maximum generosity in facilitating such a mass movement of peoples. He was a founder-member of the American Colonization Society, which was formed for this purpose.

How was his advice received?

The US obtained, in 1822, the territory of Liberia as a West African haven for returning ex-slaves. The name Liberia was a symbol of their emancipation, and the country's motto became 'We came here for freedom's sake'. Unfortunately (as in each case where this has been done), the need of the immigrants for a homeland took precedence over the rights of those people already there, who had no say in how their territory was disposed of. Alas, the experiment had unexpectedly perverse results. The freed slaves rapidly enslaved the local population. In 1930, Liberia was censured by the League of Nations for condoning 'conditions hardly distinguishable from slave-raiding and slave-trading'.[3] The civil wars that have raged in Liberia during the past decades have one root cause: the original inhabitants decided to regain control over their country.

What impact do you think the forced immigration of Africans has had on the character of America?

I agree with James Madison's conclusions. You cannot tear away from people their culture, heritage and identity without provoking a terrible reaction. Prior to the arrival of African Americans, America's immigrant population seemed likely to develop into a nation. They had come to America of their own free will and they were inspired by the ideal of a free and classless society, the shining city on the hill. They had freely decided to discard much of their original heritage and to sever their ancestral roots. They commingled with ease. Of course, there were exceptions. Some communities tended to marry among themselves. But the typical southern white American shares German, Anglo-Saxon, Scottish and Irish ancestors. Between 1820 and 1860 nine out of ten European immigrants came from England, Ireland or Germany.[4] Obviously, for all the reasons foreseen by Madison, the relationship between African and European Americans was very much more difficult.

The year 1965 was another turning point. It was then that the Immigration and Nationality Act

Amendments were passed. They abolished the policy which, previously, had organized immigration in a manner that reflected the pattern of cultural origin already established in America. The law was symbolic because, instead of continuing to favour European immigration, America had decided to become its own free world. During the 1950s there were nine times as many European immigrants as there were Asians.[5] Following the passage of the new Immigration Act, the proportions were sharply reversed. By 1990 the absolute number of immigrants from Europe had halved, whereas immigration from other continents and cultures had soared.[6] By opening itself to all those seeking freedom whatever their origins, America had decided to initiate a vast and welcoming new form of society. President Reagan, in his famous New Year's speech of 1982, described America in these terms: 'We're a nation composed of people who have come here from every corner of the world, people of all races and creeds . . .'[7]

Great enthusiasm was expressed for such a grand vision. Not only was it immensely generous in spirit, but it seemed to promise a vigorous, innovative and industrious new generation which would bring tremendous vitality to America. And so it has turned out. These immigrants now often lead the pack in school results, in research, in

science and in mathematics. But, inevitably, there
have been other consequences. As *Time* magazine
wrote: 'by 2020 . . . the number of US residents
who are Hispanic or non-white will have more
than doubled to nearly 115 million.' Only a short
time later, the population of European descent will
be a minority; 'the average US resident, as defined
by census statistics, will trace his or her descent to
Africa, Asia, the Hispanic world, the Pacific
islands, Arabia – almost anywhere but white
Europe.'[8]

What will be the consequences of these changes?

This radical transformation of the population of
America has taken place with incredible speed.
There has been large-scale legal as well as illegal
immigration (the latter estimated at between 2 and
3 million each year).[9] What is more, the immigrant
peoples, once installed, have a higher birth-rate. The
twentieth-century writers Oakeshott[10] and Santayana[11] believed that one of the disasters which
can befall any community is that its shared under-
standings, in other words its common culture, be
dissipated in too rapid or too sweeping change.

Whatever the outcome of this extraordinary and
grand experiment, it will be impossible to avoid
social torment. The destabilization and in some

cases social breakdown of the cities, the multi-ethnic, multi-tongued population, the rapid geographic mobility which has resulted in uprooted nuclear or broken families, have all contributed to widespread disorientation. As must be expected, reactions to these fast-changing conditions have been diverse. Some have sought their historic roots in Africa, Ireland, Israel, Italy, China or wherever, forming somewhat separate communities and choosing to live among themselves. They strive to preserve or to recover their cultures, religions and language. In other words, their reaction has been to respect and to protect their differences.

Others have gone in an entirely opposite direction. They have sought to eliminate diversity and to build a homogenized society by denying the existence of cultural, ethnic and even gender differences. Homogenization has brought into question the differences between men and women. It is the fact that men and women are different, that the weaknesses of one are compensated by the strengths of the other, that allow a family to live in harmony. Replacing the natural complementarity of men and women by competition between them will change society − particularly in a culture in which it is fashionable to emphasize the individual. Modern individualism regards all social structures and obligations, even those created by the family, as impediments to self-realization, and therefore as forms of oppression.

These social phenomena, homogenization of the genders and modern individualism, will further threaten the stability of the family.

What do you conclude from all this?

From a geopolitical point of view, America will find it more difficult to achieve internal agreement on its policies. Asian, Hispanic and African Americans will not respond to the special relationship with Europe as do European Americans. Similarly, European Americans will have a different attitude towards problems in other parts of the world. So American governments may attempt to create a consensus by justifying their foreign policy on humanitarian grounds, sometimes known as 'gunboat compassion', and that can rapidly degenerate into a form of neo-colonialism.

Let's now turn to the construction of Europe. You believe in a European Community, but you reject the Europe that would result from the Treaty of Maastricht. Why?

Maastricht seeks to create a supranational, centralized, bureaucratic state – a homogenized union. It would destroy the pillars on which Europe was built – its nations. It would convert Europe into one multicultural space, in which national identities would be fused and sovereignty abandoned. It would coerce ancient European nations to merge into the ultimate artificial state. As George Orwell remarked, it is characteristic of intellectuals to pass over in incomprehension the dominant political passion of the age.[12] Today, that passion is the search for national identity. And this is the moment when European ruling elites are seeking to destroy the identity of every European nation.

How is it that the peoples of twelve European nations have agreed to this?

The European Union was built in secret: not through carelessness or casualness, but in a deliberately planned and skilfully executed manner. Claude Cheysson, the former French Minister of Foreign Affairs and a member of the European Commission from 1985 to 1989, described the mechanism in an interview in *Le Figaro* on 7 May 1994.[13] He explained proudly that the European Union could only have been constructed in the absence of democracy, and he went on to suggest that the present problems were the result of having mistakenly allowed a public debate on the merits of the Treaty of Maastricht.

The British newspaper the *Guardian* lodged a case before the European Court of Justice in Luxembourg complaining of the secrecy in which European decisions are taken. Lawyers for the European Council of Ministers responded by stating to the judges that 'there is no principle of community law which gives citizens the right to EU documents.' They went on to make the astounding claim that although heads of government had repeatedly called for more openness in EU affairs, their declarations 'were of an eminently political nature and not binding on the community institutions'.[14] So they asked the judges to ignore the repeated declarations at EU summit meetings in the past two years in favour of greater openness. Statements by the twelve heads of government were no more than 'policy orientations' and had no binding effect.

This belief that the nomenklatura knows best and that the public is no more than a hindrance explains why there now exists a profound and dangerous divorce between European societies and their governing elites.

What was done in secret?

Quietly and progressively, power was transferred

to the seventeen unelected technocrats who were the members of the European Commission. Originally, power had been entrusted to the Council of Ministers, which consists of the elected national heads of state or their representatives. As they were more interested in national policies than in the creation of Europe, bit by bit the technocrats of the Commission were allowed to take over executive power. They have been granted the monopoly right to propose new initiatives for the development of the European Union. Their ambition is not modest. Jacques Delors, the outgoing president of the Commission, declared that in future 80 per cent of all laws governing economic, social and fiscal affairs of each European nation would originate in Brussels and therefore from proposals initiated by the Commission.[15]

As was certain to be the case, this rush towards technocratic hypercentralization has created a Europe which is hopelessly weak externally and unable to influence the course of world events. Internally, the power of the technocracy is employed to destroy sovereignty, freedom and self-reliance.

How do you define a technocrat?

Usually a technocrat is an ex-politician or a civil servant. He is unelected, virtually impossible to dislodge during his term of employment, and has been granted extensive executive and even legislative power without popular mandate and without being directly answerable to the people whose interests, theoretically, he is supposed to represent.

What kind of Europe do you believe in?

It would be built on the strengths, cultures and heritage of its constituent nations. The fundamental principle which would guide its institutions would be that everything that can be done at family level would be entrusted to the family, everything that can be done at the local or regional or national level would be decentralized accordingly.

I believe that democracy functions properly when it is local and participatory. In a healthy democracy it is the people who decide which powers should be entrusted to their leaders. In a false democracy, it is the leaders who decide which freedoms are to be lent to the people.

When constituencies are small, their elected representatives must concern themselves with the local interests of their constituents. When political representatives are distant and faceless and represent vast numbers of unknown constituents, they represent not their constituents, but special-interest groups whose lobbyists are numerous and ever-present.

What is more, democracy should be participatory and not just representative. By that I mean that citizens should retain the final decision on matters which will significantly affect their society. In a functioning democracy such as Switzerland, 100,000 people are entitled to call a national referendum on any issue concerning changes in the constitution. A petition signed by 50,000 people can insist that proposals presented to Parliament be submitted to a public referendum. But in Great Britain, for example, the government has systematically refused to allow a referendum on the Treaty of Maastricht, a treaty that radically diminishes national sovereignty. The government's excuse is that referenda are not part of the British political system. And yet when Britain originally joined the European Community, the British people *were* given the opportunity to express their opinion in a national referendum. No, the real reason is that opinion polls show that Maastricht would be resoundingly rejected by the British people. By refusing to allow a free vote on so vital an issue, the present government is demonstrating its contempt for the people who elected it.

Participatory democracy is a way of controlling the power of politicians once they have been elected; it also ensures that ultimate responsibility remains with the electorate. The right to call a referendum should be available both at the local and at the national level.

But European leaders have always accepted the principle of subsidiarity and stated that they would seek optimum decentralization.

Subsidiarity has been used by the Eurocrats to mask their lust for centralization. It is supposed to mean optimum decentralization of power, but the word itself is now hopelessly discredited. What a farce it has been to witness the Commission claiming that they are acting according to the spirit of subsidiarity while at the same time predicting that 80 per cent of all national laws will originate in Brussels!

What areas of responsibility should concern Brussels?

Principally defence, diplomacy, protection of the environment and maintaining a free internal market within Europe.

What institutions would be necessary for this purpose?

The principal executive institution should be the European Council of Ministers which, as I have said, consists of the elected national heads of state and their representatives. Because under the present system the representative of each European country in turn becomes president of the Council for a few months, a vice-president of the Council should be appointed and would be responsible to the members. This would ensure executive continuity. Otherwise, as we have seen, the unelected technocrats of the Commission fill the void.

What about the European Commission?

It should be the administrative secretariat of the Council. It should be stripped of executive and legislative power and expected to work in the efficient and disciplined manner which a democracy expects from its functionaries.

What structures would be needed for defence and diplomacy?

They should be entrusted to a European Security Council not too dissimilar to the UN Security Council. The large European nations, which would provide the bulk of military capacity, would be the principal members of the Security Council. All European nations would be free to opt out of military initiatives decided on by the European Security Council. The Council would be able to draw on the armed forces of those nations which agree to participate, without seeking to create a homogenized Euro-corps. The development and production of military equipment could be carried out in a coordinated manner through joint ventures between European corporations.

The principal purpose of Europe's defence must be to protect Europe's vital interests and, more particularly, to defend its territory against military or uncontrolled invasion. It should not pursue neo-colonial expeditions under the guise of humanitarian aid, whose real purpose is often to help some western politician's career at home.

What do you mean by uncontrolled invasion?

I mean immigration on a scale which cannot be integrated.

And what should be the relationship between the European Security Council, the USA and NATO?

Now that the Cold War is over, Europe must

grow up. It is absurd that 250 million Americans should be asked to defend 350 million Europeans against an unknown enemy. Europe and the USA should work as independent allies and NATO could be the structure used for ad hoc cooperation.

And the environment?

Environmental problems do not respect frontiers, therefore standards should be established at the European level and applied throughout Europe. European diplomacy should seek to obtain international acceptance of these standards. And, of course, environmental disasters must be prevented where possible or tackled by prompt and effective international action.

What role do you see for the European Parliament?

Before discussing the Parliament, I would like to describe one final European institution which I believe to be vitally important. All organizations, as they degenerate, become centralized and bureaucratic. The Founding Fathers, in Philadelphia, originally conceived the United States as a true federation of free peoples. James Buchanan, the American Nobel Prize-winning economist, suggested recently that America has evolved into a state not much different from other centralized states, and that James Madison could never have believed that his concept of federalism would degenerate into a centralized leviathan.[16]

The supreme duty of the new institution would be to prohibit the accumulation of power by the centre. Decentralization must be the fundamental principle on which Europe is built.

As for the European Parliament, it is a pseudo-democratic institution. It is totally dominated by the two major parties, the Socialists and the Christian Democrats, both of which share with the European Commission the vision of a supra-national, centralized European state dominating a homogenized union. Its only real function is to provide cover for the Commission.

When the European Council of Ministers and the Commission are in disagreement, the confrontation is clearly and embarrassingly defined: it is the technocrats of Brussels versus the elected representatives of the nations. In such a contest, the European Parliament is the natural ally of the technocrats. As I have said, they share the same objectives. What is more, they can only achieve those objectives by subjugating the national parliaments. The strength of the European

Parliament and the Commission is in inverse proportion to that of the national democratic institutions. The weaker the national institutions, the stronger are those of Brussels. So the European Commission and the European Parliament share both the same objectives and the same enemy.

Under your plan, what powers should be granted to the European Parliament?

Its authority should be limited to overseeing those few matters that need to be centralized.

The European Parliament already has the right to ratify treaties between the European Union and third parties, as well as the right to ratify the acceptance of new nations into the Union. Those powers seem acceptable. In addition, it should have the right to approve senior appointments to European institutions. It has been granted the right to approve the membership of the Commission, but at the moment it exercises that right irresponsibly. It votes without appropriate knowledge. There are no public confirmation hearings and, as a result, neither Members of Parliament nor the public are given the opportunity to learn about the candidates.

What about control of the European budget?

The Parliament already has the duty to approve the European central budget as well as to vote a discharge for the year-end accounts. This is equivalent to approving the annual accounts of a corporation during the annual meeting of shareholders. But here is another example of the Parliament's impotence. The European accounts for the years 1982 and 1992 were rejected for gross irregularities. You would have thought that such a condemnation would be a major event with major consequences. Not at all. The accounts have remained unapproved and the Commission continues to distribute funds at an accelerating pace.

What other powers should the European Parliament be granted?

I realize that I have supplied examples rather than an exhaustive list, but at the moment the work of the European Parliament is overwhelmingly either a waste of time or downright destructive. In this latter category I include all the legislation and discussion papers concerning matters which are none of the European Parliament's business because they should be the responsibility of national parliaments. We should be extremely circumspect in granting powers to this Parliament. When you pay nearly 600 people to pass laws, they pass laws, and most of them are, at best, useless.

You are an opponent of the project for a single currency. Why?

The effects of a single currency go far beyond the economy. They would transform the political structure of Europe as well as the stability of its societies.

A currency is both an economic tool and a reflection of the economic and social condition of a society. The quantity of available money must be determined in a way which does not lead to unacceptable levels of inflation, deflation or other disruptions. Obviously, a single currency would have to be managed centrally, and that necessarily would mean that the principal economic strategy of each European nation would also need to be determined centrally. It would be impossible to have a single currency while at the same time maintaining different economic programmes in each of twelve nations.

The true purpose of proposing a single currency is to force through the creation of a unitary

European state while pretending to promote a purely economic idea. It is yet another example of the Eurocrats acting by stealth so as to achieve their aim of a homogenized European union.

Furthermore, a single currency would disrupt European societies. To understand the effects of a single currency imposed uniformly on both rich and poor regions, look at Italy.

The economy of northern Italy is highly competitive compared to the remainder of Europe, whereas that of the south is not. Obviously, the currency used in the south cannot be adjusted relative to that of the north in order to reflect the differences in their economies because the south and the north maintain the same currency. The economy in the south stagnated and unemployment increased. Unemployed southerners moved north to seek work and to stem this migration Italy subsidized investment in the south to create jobs. To do this, special institutions were formed such as the Cassa del Mezzogiorno and its successors, through which were channelled massive transfers of funds to the south. The policy failed. Much of the investment went into useless bureaucratic mega-projects and much was stolen or diverted for political purposes. Instead of generating employment, the subsidies generated corruption. They also failed to stop migration, which continued to uproot southern communities and to overpopulate and destabilize those in the north. This is a typical case of mutual poisoning. Families and communities in the south are destroyed and urban slums and social crisis develop in the north.

This fiasco caused great resentment in northern Italy, resulting in the formation of the Lombardy League, whose platform is to re-establish autonomy for the north. The League has become an important political movement and is part of the present governing coalition.

These subsidies and migrations took place within the same nation, yet they aroused strong separatist passions. Imagine how much greater would be the resentment if they took place between different nations, such as Greece and the Netherlands or Spain and Germany. Undoubtedly, there would be great tensions if at some time in the future Greece and Spain – or indeed any other nation – were unable to maintain the standards of economic stability prevalent in the Netherlands or Germany. With a single currency, no individual nation would be able to adjust the value of its currency to reflect its own economic realities. The results would be the same as in Italy, but on a much larger and more devastating scale: uprooting of the peoples of unsuccessful nations; mass migration; destabilization of the towns in successful nations; emergence of centrifugal forces which could create possibly violent separatist movements and pull Europe apart.

The Eurocrats understand this, and included in the Treaty of Maastricht two articles, Articles 123 and 130C, along with a special protocol on 'Economic and Social Cohesion'. The purpose of these measures is to reproduce, on a Europe-wide scale, a complex of institutions like the Cassa del Mezzogiorno. There is no reason to suppose that the results would not be the same.

Even so, and despite all the instability in the world, the Eurocrats still believe that people must move to jobs, and not jobs to people. This confirms their deep ignorance of how societies function. In a stable society, all members of a family together with their friends and neighbours create the public opinion which guides the behaviour of children as they grow up to take their place in society. But if, to find work, the mother, father and children are forced to move, the influences that help to educate the children are transformed. The elders who have been left behind regroup into special retirement cities. Often the responsibility for shaping a child's values is transferred to schools which themselves are in deep moral crisis. The children become anonymous members of impersonal communities, with no relatives to take the place of parents who are out at work. In particularly severe cases, when families break down the children seek surrogate families in urban gangs.

A true city is not an encampment for transient visitors, nor a complex of motorways, nor an ephemeral agglomeration of living quarters. It is a long-standing human settlement, a community spanning generations, a complex social organization inspiring commitment and pride. Every architectural blight, every symptom of social breakdown, should pierce deep into the heart of its citizens and provoke a salutary reaction. Siena, in Italy, is perhaps the best example of a healthy city. That is why it has maintained social stability and a negligible incidence of crime.

What are your proposals for a European currency?

I believe that each nation should maintain its own currency which would be convertible at a fixed rate into the Ecu. The Ecu would be run by the European Central Bank whose task would be to maintain its value and to ensure that devaluations or revaluations of national currencies would not be predatory in nature, but as far as possible reflections of economic reality. The Ecu would be managed as a pure reserve currency rather than as a domestic currency, which by nature responds to local economic and political expediency.

The difference between a single and a common currency is that a single currency is fixed, inflexible and incapable of adjusting to the economic realities of each nation. A common currency is supple, and can respond to the changes that will inevitably affect national economies.

Your idea seems very similar to the British proposal for the hard Ecu.

It is, in many regards. In fact, I first proposed this common currency on 12 June 1990, when I was invited to deliver the Institute of Directors' Annual Lecture in London. The British government's plan was published in October 1990. This is not to say that I am claiming paternity. Very often an idea is in the air and several people are convinced by it more or less simultaneously.

What sort of Europe does Germany want?

The governing party, the Christian Democrats, published in September 1994 what it calls its 'Reflections on European Policy'.[17]

The objective is unequivocal: to create an integrated state; to convert the European Parliament into a typical national law-making institution appropriate for a unitary state; to transform the Council of Ministers into a second parliamentary chamber; and to allow the Commission to become the executive European government. The new European supra-state would be built on the doctrine of global free trade. It would expand to include the nations of Central and Eastern Europe and would develop a wide-ranging partnership with Russia. Of course, at the centre of Europe would be Germany, the colossus in the landscape.

Is it still possible to change the course of the European Union or are we committed to a supranational union?

In 1996, there will be an inter-governmental conference to reconsider the structures of Europe. That will be the time to mount an all-out effort to change course. The battle will take place at the national level. In every European nation, political coalitions will be formed to fight for a new Treaty based on a Europe of nations. And they will have to do whatever is necessary to ensure that the final decision is taken democratically. That means a national referendum in each European nation.

THE TRAP

Are small nations still viable?

Of course they are. Local democracy, which is naturally inherent in a small democratic nation, is far superior to the distant democracy of mega-states. The societies of small democratic nations have the opportunity to be infinitely more stable than those of the mega-states, in which much of the population is rootless and anonymous.

Small nations have obvious disadvantages in terms of defence and diplomacy. Also, they may need access to a large homogeneous free market which can provide the competitive conditions that modern economies seem to demand. But, as we have seen, a decentralized European Community consisting of a family of nations can supply the requisite defence and diplomatic strength as well as a large free market without destroying the identity and autonomy of small constituent nations.

Modern thinkers have forgotten that cultural affinity is a necessary precondition of political allegiance.

In any case the vast, centralized, multicultural nations have not demonstrated that their structures are viable. The Soviet Union has collapsed. And the United States has become a leviathan, partially paralyzed by its centralization.

What about the new world order?

We've certainly heard a lot about it. In my view, it should ensure that each nation is entitled to pursue peacefully its own way of life with its own culture and traditions, even if they seem exotic or inconceivable to us. The bedrock of social diversity is mutual respect. As we look around within our own western communities and see our own disarray, we should be willing to behave towards others with humility.

4

Rethinking the
Welfare State

Many developed nations are reconsidering the structures of their systems of welfare. What is your view?

The universal welfare state cannot be sustained. Its economic costs and its social consequences are unbearable.

The rightful purpose of institutionalized state welfare should be to supply a safety net to those who need it. It should not be to eliminate the natural responsibilities of citizens, families, local communities, religious communities and other structures which, in a healthy society, intervene at different levels between the individual and the state.

Those who wish to destroy the conditions which allow for a strong democratic nation can do little better than to reduce the self-reliance of citizens and of their families by converting them into dependants of the state. Inevitably the result is the strengthening of state bureaucracy and the weakening of civil society.

Earlier, when discussing the construction of

Europe, we talked about the word 'subsidiarity' and what it is supposed to represent. It should mean leaving to the family everything that can be done at family level; leaving to local, social or religious communities everything that can be done at the local level; leaving to the region everything that can be done regionally; and only putting into the hands of the state bureaucracy those responsibilities which cannot be decentralized.

The idea that society consists of a multitude of individuals is wrong. In reality a robust society consists of families and local communities. These are the true building blocks, and it is these essential elements of society that the universal welfare state weakens by reducing their responsibilities and their authority. If you remove from a family its duty to provide for the health, education and welfare of its children, you destroy the cohesion of that family and thereby the community to which it belongs. The children effectively become wards of the state.

Far-reaching reforms will need to be proposed so as to alter the fundamental orientation of state intervention. These can only be carried through following a national debate and a referendum. In a free society major changes such as these must have the legitimacy of public endorsement.

THE TRAP

Let's start with your proposals for the health service.

A prosperous and civilized society must ensure that all its citizens have access to decent medical services. The question therefore concerns the means rather than the objective.

The way in which medical services are provided should be based on the twin principles of subsidiarity and diversity. As it is imperative that local communities survive, indeed prosper, without their populations being swept into the major urban concentrations, they must have access to local hospitals, which should be able to treat relatively widespread and predictable illnesses. Centralization is necessary for highly sophisticated and specialized services which, in order to be reasonably economic, need to cover a much wider area. Local hospitals would send to the specialized hospitals those patients who need particular care. Thus the siting of hospitals should follow a double movement: decentralization for standard hospitals and centralization for highly specialized establishments.

The purpose of diversity in medical services is to provide choice and to improve quality by introducing an element of competition while maintaining and improving the national system in those countries in which it already exists. There should be a multitude of hospitals run variously by doctors' cooperatives, religious communities, local communities, charities and private enterprise, as well as the services run by the state where they exist.

The state would retain a major role. There should be legislation requiring that everyone, at birth, be insured for health. That insurance must be for life so as to make it illegal for insurers to exclude anyone as a result of some subsequent deterioration in his or her health. As everyone would be insured for life, medical differences at birth would be in the price. Insurance premiums would be priced so as to cater for the normal pattern of human health at birth and therefore would be the same for everyone for the rest of their lives.

Those providing the insurance could be both private and state insurers, the latter more particularly in those nations where national health insurance is already in place. The state service would provide an extra layer of choice and competition.

Mandatory insurance should not be shocking. It already exists. If you drive a car, by law you must insure against third-party risks. And in many countries which now provide a National Health

Service, mandatory health insurance is already in practice. The payments for social security are deducted automatically from wages and passed to the state system.

The state would intervene by paying the insurance premiums of those people who cannot afford them. In this way the state would concentrate its financial support on those who need it and would not convert self-reliant citizens into dependants. This would liberate very substantial funds to be deployed to improve medical services. Without such a radical change, the quality of state-provided services will continue to deteriorate unacceptably. The funds are just not available for it to be otherwise.

The public could continue to use the national system, which would be much improved as funds are freed to be used for investment. And the public would also have the option to choose among all the other hospitals and medical services that would emerge, in a free market, alongside the state service.

Those hospitals and medical services that best satisfy the public would expand. Those which do not satisfy would have to improve their performance, or else ultimately disappear. The public would be the winner.

How could you be certain that private insurance companies are able to honour their commitments?

That is another role for the state. It must make certain that the private insurers are satisfactorily financed and prudently managed. Also, there should be some sort of industry-wide insurance system guaranteeing the commitments of each insurer.

Many believe in equal access to medical services. Doesn't the system that you recommend create two tiers of medicine, one for the rich and the other for the poor?

What I am suggesting is that the rich pay for themselves and that the poor obtain help from the community. Both have access to a choice of state and private hospitals and medical services. It is up to each society to determine the minimum levels of health care that it wishes to guarantee to its people.

How would the price of pharmaceutical products and medical services be kept under control?

Let's start with pharmaceutical products. Generally speaking, two different systems exist for controlling prices: on the one hand formal controls exercised by the state, and on the other the control which results from a competitive free market. In such a market, true competition between numerous producers automatically forces them to compete both on quality and on price. Of course, it is this latter system which prevails in the USA, the UK and many other countries which believe in free markets.

Unfortunately, in the case of pharmaceutical products, this concept is based on a false premise. The markets are not free but, on the contrary, are monopolistic. Producers are unable to act independently and competitively one against the other. The reason is that the corporation which develops a new product obtains an exclusive patent, providing it with a long-lasting monopoly.

The patent-holder is free to sell his product at any price that he determines. If the product has unique qualities and, for example, is the best medicine available to treat a particular and dangerous disease, you are forced to buy it at whatever price is charged. That is why the profit margins on pharmaceutical products are astronomically and unacceptably high.

The justification for such profits is that if research is not properly rewarded it will cease, and that if research is halted the public will no longer benefit from medical innovation. That is true. But a solution is available which motivates and rewards research while at the same time eliminating excessive abuse of the public, or, in the case of nationalized health services, the state.

Patents would continue to be issued. When a new product is developed, the developer would receive a patent. But any bona fide manufacturer of pharmaceutical products would automatically be entitled to obtain a licence from the patentholder to produce the new product and would pay a fixed royalty for the privilege. In other words, the creator would receive a significant part of the funds spent by the public on buying his creation, no matter which company manufactures the final product.

In this way, research would be well remunerated and motivated, and real competition would be introduced to the marketplace. Numerous manufacturers could produce the new product; they would all pay the same percentage of their sales as a royalty; and they would compete vigorously both on quality and on price. This would result in a sharp drop in the price of medicines. The state would be responsible for ensuring minimum quality standards which all would have to respect and it would make certain that no secret cartel arrangements inhibited freedom of the market.

What about the prices of medical services?

Prices would be controlled to some degree by the normal commercial pressures exercised by the insurers. In addition, as in Germany, medical authorities would establish price guidelines. Finally, as health services are of such importance, there should be a formal system of arbitration which would settle differences between insurers and the suppliers of medical services.

What about education?

The same general principles are valid for education as for health. Both must be based on subsidiarity and diversity. In the case of education, there must also be a large measure of family control over state schools.

By subsidiarity, I mean maximum decentralization so that schools are deeply embedded in local communities. By diversity, I mean that, side by side, there should be a multitude of types of schools: those run by the state, the municipalities, local communities, religious communities, teachers' cooperatives, parents' cooperatives, private enterprise, etc. This would provide choice for parents. The consequence, as usual in a free market, would be that those schools which satisfy the public would expand and those which do not would either reform their operations or contract. The state would supply vouchers to families which could be used in the school of their choice. The vouchers would need to be of sufficient value so that well-managed schools, when they cash them in, would receive enough funds to enable them to maintain standards as well as to be profitable.

Additionally, the state should establish norms for basic levels of education, examinations and standards of hygiene in schools. The norms would be the minimum acceptable to society and, as competition between different schools emerges, they should in practice be much improved upon.

Would the vouchers be free for all families?

That is a question for each society to decide. For my part, I believe that they should be free for poor families, but not for the rich. But it would be very important that there be no distinction among vouchers. The fact that one voucher was free and the other was paid for should not even be made known to the school itself.

Insofar as higher education is concerned, state payments should be by way of loans which students would repay. The rate of repayment could be set at a fixed percentage of their subsequent earnings.

If such a system were adopted, it would free up very considerable funds to improve educational services.

Have you any other recommendations for education?

I don't think it is right that the speed of progress of the more gifted students should be linked to that of those who cannot keep up with the average level of the class. This is as true for academic studies as it is for sports or the arts.

Also, I am a firm believer in apprenticeship. Education should be based on both theoretical studies and practical experience. I know many well-meaning and capable teachers who have a serious deficiency. At no time are their ideas confronted with the real world.

Those who practise a discipline, rather than merely teaching it, are constantly testing their ideas in the real world and, very quickly, if the ideas seem to be failing, changing them until a successful system is found. A theoretician can continue to believe in and teach the same theories without ever discovering whether they are effective. This is like the legendary character, Virtuoso, who considers himself an expert on all things that move and believes that he is the world's greatest swimmer. He demonstrates the strokes while lying on a table but never swims in the water.

Most western societies are constantly losing knowledge and valuable skills. Instead of an apprentice learning reality from a master, we have students learning theory from a theoretician. Germany has gained a great advantage over its European competitors by maintaining its respect for apprenticeship.

What about the other aspects of the universal welfare state?

We need to go back to the beginning and redefine our objectives. It seems to me that the purpose of state welfare is to provide a safety net for those who temporarily or permanently are incapable of looking after themselves. It should not be a bureaucratic appropriation of a citizen's natural responsibilities from the cradle to the coffin. It should not take over the individual need to provide for one's family and for retirement and to insure against the risks of ill-health.

We have witnessed where such a policy leads. The Swedish model of welfare resulted in a system in which it was possible to earn as much by not working as by working: fathers of new-born children could obtain one year's paid paternity leave; and paid absenteeism on medical and psychological grounds became commonplace with substantial proportions of the workforce routinely not turning up for work. In the Netherlands, a shrewd worker can retire at forty-three on full salary.

Professor Walter Williams of George Mason University has shown that fundamental problems are not solved by merely throwing money at them. For example, he writes: 'The money spent on poverty programmes since the 1960s could have bought the entire assets of the Fortune 500 companies and virtually all the US farmland. And what did it do? The problems still remain and they are worse.'[1]

Our problem is clear. For decades we have defined our system of welfare without any thought as to why the need for welfare develops or how we should provide support without destroying the moral fibre of those who receive it and without destabilizing society as a whole. Our action has sometimes been generous in intent, but more often it has been motivated by political expediency and by weakness. Today our welfare system accommodates the failings of our society without ever addressing them. We alleviate the symptoms of our social disorientation while aggravating its fundamental causes.

5

Modern Agriculture and the Destruction of Society

You believe that intensive farming, on which modern agriculture is based, damages public health and destabilizes society. Why?

Intensive farming is based on the belief that food is like any other product and that agriculture will respond to technology in the same way as industry does. If new technology is introduced, the argument goes, enhanced efficiency and productivity will follow. Large, mechanized modern farms using the latest scientific discoveries will produce more food, more cheaply, for the benefit of the economy and of people throughout the world. The necessary elimination of rural jobs, the reasoning continues, is no different from the daily loss of industrial jobs due to technological innovation. What is more, men and women will be liberated from the land and made free to participate in the dynamic sectors of contemporary industry, where they will contribute to the growth of GNP and to public prosperity.

At first sight this seems obvious. Yet it is totally wrong. When people leave the land, they gravitate to the cities in search of work. But throughout the world there are not enough urban jobs and the infrastructure – such as lodgings, schools, hospitals, etc. – is already insufficient. The result is increased unemployment, with the attendant costs of welfare, as well as a need for substantial expenditure on infrastructure. These are the indirect costs of intensive agriculture and they must be taken into account.

There is also a deeper price. When, as a result of change, jobs are lost in a particular industry the fundamental balance of society is not altered. Some declining companies necessarily suffer while other, more competitive entities emerge. But loss of rural employment and migration from the countryside to the cities causes a fundamental and irreversible shift. It has contributed throughout the world to the destabilization of rural society and to the growth of vast urban concentrations. In the urban slums congregate uprooted individuals whose families have been splintered, whose cultural traditions have been extinguished and who have been reduced to dependence on welfare from the state. They form an alienated underclass. From the first world to the third, these huge shantytowns have become tragic, morbid intumescences. The cost of such social breakdown can never be measured. The damage is too fundamental. Throughout the world social breakdown in the mega-cities threatens the existence of free societies.

THE TRAP

As José Lutzenberger, the far-sighted former Environment Minister of Brazil, writes,[1] the notorious slums of Brazil, known as *favelas*, were the direct result of the rural dislocations caused by the Green Revolution of the 1950s. This was the first major scientific initiative to apply intensive farming to a large area. It was supposed to end, for all time, famine throughout the world.

But do you question the assertion that intensive agriculture is more productive?

The only measure by which large farms are more productive is in the use of labour. If productivity is measured in terms of production per acre, or per unit of energy, or relative capital input, it is the small farm which comes out best.[2]

Output per person might have been an important consideration in the highly developed western nations, where the cost of labour is great and standards of living are high. But we are entering a new world in which we must accommodate 4 billion people who have suddenly joined the world economy, including the populations of China, India, Vietnam, Bangladesh and countries of the ex-Soviet Union among others. These populations are growing fast, and are forecast to reach 6.5 billion in thirty-five years. Under these new circumstances, the question is no longer how to save labour. The problem is how to stabilize these vast and fast-growing populations, a very large part of them unemployed.

Take Vietnam as an example. It has a population of 74 million of whom 80 per cent live in the countryside (compared to 14.8 per cent in Australia, a major agricultural country).[3] Driving them from the fields into urban slums would create devastation.

In the world as a whole, there are still 3.1 billion people living in the countryside. If intensive methods of agriculture were imposed universally and productivity per person were to reach the levels of Australia, then, as we have discussed, about 2 billion of these people will lose their livelihood. Rural communities throughout the world would be washed away as if by a great flood. Whole populations would be uprooted and swept into urban slums. As the affected nations become ungovernable and impoverished, so their people would be forced to seek refuge elsewhere. Mass migrations of displaced people would follow. Yet economists totally disregard these social and economic costs when they calculate the cost of food produced by intensive methods.

Modern society believes in intensive farming because modern culture is based on measuring and counting rather than on trying to understand longer-term and more important consequences.

What are the other effects of intensive farming?

Its effects on the environment and on the public are well known: soil erosion, water pollution by chemical effluents, accelerated depletion of ground water, destruction of genetic diversity, pollution of foodstuffs and damage to public health.

You talk of the effects on public health of intensively produced food. What do you have in mind?

The purpose of intensive rearing of animals is to achieve the greatest weight gain over the shortest period of time for the lowest cost. It seeks weight gain not nutrient gain, and that is achieved most easily by putting on fat rather than protein. At present chickens, turkeys, ducks, pigs, veal calves and beef cattle are commonly reared by intensive methods. Salmon, trout, halibut and some other fish are more recent recruits.

As an example I will take the meat which was first produced by modern factory farming, chicken.

Broilers, typically, are reared in sheds each containing 40,000 growing birds. There are eight crops per year, so eight times each year 40,000 one- or two-day-old chicks are delivered to each shed from incubators in a hatchery. There they will remain until they are ready for slaughter, forty-two days later. Their feed contains very little natural vegetable material, but instead consists of a considerable proportion of fish meal and what is discreetly called 'bone meal'. This, in fact, is the remains of previous generations of their own and other species. In many cases, to their feed will be added artificial growth promoters such as antibiotics (virginiamycin, for example) and anticoccidials to treat fungal infections. Regular feeding of antibiotics to intensively reared animals produces an additional weight gain of perhaps 5 per cent.[4] Similar industrial processes are applied to other animals.

Intensively reared animals are physically different from their free-living counterparts. In the meat of free animals, the protein content far exceeds the fat content. In intensively reared animals the proportion of fat to protein is much higher. After converting the figures to their calorific value, the ratio of fat to protein is often found to be nine times greater in domestically reared animals than in their free counterparts. In chicken, it has been demonstrated that since the end of the last century the carcass fat content has risen by nearly 1,000 per cent.[5]

The change goes further. Generally speaking

there are three main types of fat, two of which concern us most – polyunsaturated and saturated. Polyunsaturated fat includes essential fatty acids, so called because they are essential for the growth and development of the brain and are components of all cell membranes which need them in order to function effectively. They help to produce hormone-like substances which regulate, among other things, the immune and vascular systems. Saturated fats, on the other hand, are a significant contributory factor in heart disease and possibly also a factor in breast and colon cancer.[6]

Wild pigs are expected to have twice the concentration of essential fatty acids as of saturated fat. In contrast, the modern pig has five times more saturated fat than polyunsaturated fat – a transformation by a factor of ten times, the wrong way.[7]

So the damage to the value of our food is twofold: the meat will contain relatively more fat than protein, and the quality of that fat will have been perverted.

There is still more. The limited space in which the animals live facilitates the transmission of microbes which increases the spread of infection. The unnatural living conditions are themselves likely to damage the animals' health and reduce their resistance to disease. And as the animals are bred from uniform genetic stock constituting a form of monoculture, they are all vulnerable to the same infections. Vaccines, antibiotics and other drugs are administered to prevent epidemics. The systematic use of antibiotics may create resistant bacteria, which can then spread to man.[8]

Is mad cow disease connected to intensive rearing of animals?

Mad cow disease or bovine spongiform encephalopathy (BSE) is one of a group of infectious diseases known as TSEs: transmissible spongiform encephalopathies. The TSE which affects sheep is called scrapie and the form which principally affects humans is known as Creutzfeldt-Jakob disease. The diseases are always fatal and there is no known treatment. They are transmissible to other species, have very long incubation periods and are present in many tissues of the animal's body long before symptoms are seen. They act by causing the disintegration of cells throughout the brain and replacing them with microscopic holes which give a spongelike appearance, hence the name 'spongiform'.

The disease is transmitted by infectious agents whose chemical nature is still unknown. They are very small, smaller than all classified viruses, and there is no way of identifying infected animals before they have developed symptoms, except by injecting cells into mice. Even then the results may not be available for up to a year.

The infectious agents are extraordinarily tough and heat-resistant. Experiments have shown that they can survive any dose of X-rays or irradiation that is viable in practice; antiseptics or enzymes or formaldehyde; exposure to 360 degrees centigrade for one hour; and autoclaving under conditions that kill all other known infectious agents.[9] They are durable and will persist for many years in the soil.[10] Domestic cooking is not expected to have any effect on them at all.

TSEs affect mammals, but not other species (except for the long-lived ostriches). It is interesting to note that when a TSE is transferred from one species to another, the properties of the infectious agents change. For example, it seems that scrapie cannot be transmitted directly from sheep to rhesus monkeys and in light of the genetic relationship between the rhesus monkey and humans this is consistent with the view that scrapie does not directly affect man. But if scrapie is transmitted experimentally from sheep to mink, then the mink TSE develops new properties and can be experimentally transmitted to rhesus monkeys.[11] Thus it seems that TSEs can be transferred either directly or indirectly across the barriers between species.

The first cases of BSE were identified in 1986. Many scientists believe that the infectious agents were transmitted to cows through feed which contained products from rendering plants, i.e. factories that process the remains of slaughtered animals, including cows. The material they produce is added to animal feed and described variously as concentrates, protein supplements or bone meal. Thus, we are feeding cow remains to cows, in other words forcing cows into cannibalism.

It is interesting to note that in the first half of this century there was another form of TSE which affected humans – Kuru disease. It occurred in the Fore tribe, a Stone Age civilization which at the time practised cannibalism.

How did the British authorities react when BSE appeared?

The government found itself in an extremely difficult position. Evidence was slim and the risks, although great, were unproven. As there is a considerable period of incubation it would take some years to establish whether the epidemic could spread from cows to humans. A full alert by the government might have caused panic and would have had a potentially disastrous impact on British farming.

So the government reacted by establishing advisory scientific committees and taking some precautionary measures to reassure the public.

As of 1989, 'high-risk' organs were to be removed from slaughtered cattle[12] – a useful decision which might or might not be wholly successful because it has not been established where in the tissues of cattle the infectious agents settle. For example, all organs and meat contain nerves that are in physical connection with the brain. It is known that several infectious agents pass between an animal's peripheral organs and the brain by moving along the nerves. Therefore, if the brain is infected, the nerves may also be infected.

Furthermore, it was decided that cattle thought to be infected with BSE were to be reported and milk from obviously ill and infected cows was banned from sale. This was also useful but, as I have explained, there is no ready way of identifying infected animals until the disease reaches the final stages, so the effects of these decisions are necessarily limited to those animals in which the disease is already obvious.

The committees also recommended a ban on the

feeding of ruminant-based protein to ruminants. In other words, no more cannibalism to be imposed on ruminants. That was an excellent decision but the ban was not extended to pigs and poultry, which continue to be fed on the remains of their own species. In any case, the effects of this recommendation must now be reassessed as a result of the convincing evidence of maternal transmission of BSE from dams to their calves. Although contested by government scientists, it now seems almost certain that natural transmission of BSE from cow to calf has been taking place and will continue unless preventive action is taken.[13]

One of the principal conclusions, in February 1989, of the government-sponsored Southwood Committee was: 'From present evidence, it is likely that cattle will prove to be a "dead-end host" for the disease agent and most unlikely that BSE will have any implications for human health. Nevertheless, if our assessment of these likelihoods is incorrect, the implications would be extremely serious.'[14] The phrase 'dead-end host' means that the BSE stops here and will not be transferred from the cow to other species.

Do you believe that this conclusion was right?

More than five years have passed since the Southwood Report was published and the epidemic has
spread much more rapidly than predicted. Instead
of the total of 20,000 affected animals forecast by
the Committee, the figure is already above 130,000
with some 30,000 farms having experienced at
least one case of the disease (52 per cent of UK
dairy farms).[15] According to Dr Stephen Dealler of
the Department of Microbiology at York District
Hospital, this figure only represents about 20 per
cent of the animals affected, the remainder having
been eaten before the diagnosis had been carried
out.[16]

In addition, the disease has been transmitted to
seventeen out of the eighteen mammal species
which are known to have been exposed to BSE.[17]
These include the mouse, the antelope, the oryx
and the cat, as well as the pig and the marmoset
monkey. The appearance of the disease in the pig
is significant because pig tissues are similar to those
of man (various connective tissue components
from the pig have been used for human grafts).
Transmission of the disease to monkeys is
especially disquieting because of their close
relationship to humans. According to Professor
Richard Lacey of the Department of Microbiology
of the University of Leeds, 'the central tenet of the

government's reassurances that BSE cannot be a danger to man because it cannot "spread" is now completely discredited. The implications for cattle farming and probably also for human health are very grave.'[18]

Already two cases are known of beef cattle breeders who have contracted Creutzfeldt-Jakob disease, the human version of TSE. There is also a sixteen-year-old girl dying from Creutzfeldt-Jakob disease, the cause of which doctors have so far been unable to determine.[19]

BSE has now been identified in countries other than the UK, among them Canada, France, Germany, Ireland, Portugal and Denmark, where the disease is thought to have spread from imported British cattle. It was this, along with increasing concern about inter-species trans-mission, that led the German government to ques-tion the safety of British beef. The Germans tried to adopt a preventive approach to the issue, with Health Minister Horst Seehofer commenting that 'we cannot live by the slogan "Because there is no scientific knowledge we don't need to act".'[20] The German government called for a Europe-wide ban on the export of British cattle, which was fiercely resisted by the British government. When the European Commission failed to act, in June 1994 the Germans declared a unilateral six-month ban on imports of British beef, risking prosecution by the European Court of Justice. This finally forced the European Union to act on the matter, and on 18 July it was agreed to amend EU regulations on the export of cattle carcasses. British farmers are now required to certify that any beef carcasses exported to the EU have not come from a herd which has had BSE during the last six years. Previously the time period was two years, but that was not long enough to allow incubation and therefore identification of the disease.

Are these isolated incidents or should we expect other problems resulting from intensive farming?

The new frontier of intensive agriculture is bio-technology, which includes genetic manipulation. No doubt it will bring some remarkable and unexpected results.

The story of the bio-synthetic Bovine Growth Hormone is a good example of the way in which genetically engineered products destined for agricultural use are tested and presented to farmers and to the public. The chemical industry changed the name of this product to Bovine Somatotropin or BST, presumably so as to eliminate the word 'hormone', which makes the public suspicious.

Originally the industry claimed that BST, while

substantially increasing the milk production of a cow, would do so without augmenting the level of hormones in milk and without adverse or toxic effects on the health of cows. Milk produced in this way, it is claimed, is safe for humans.[21] A further attraction of using BST is that it requires little capital investment.

The initial reactions from the US Food and Drug Administration and from the UK government were positive. The British Minister of Agriculture went so far as to say: 'The idea that Britain should stand aside while allowing everyone else to produce milk in the modern way is barmy ... Nobody has any doubts about damage being done to human beings, it is totally safe.'[22]

Nonetheless there were dissenters who questioned the benefits and safety of pushing cows like high-performance machines with the aid of greater amounts of drugs.

The dissenters' case was much reinforced when documents were leaked to Samuel Epstein, Professor of Occupational and Environmental Medicine at the University of Illinois Medical Center, detailing the results of BST tests carried out in the laboratories of the Monsanto chemical group.[23] Here are a few verbatim extracts from the leaked documents:

- 'Significant increases in milk Somatotropin were noted at the five times level of treatment.' Somatotropin is the synthetic hormone in BST, which was not supposed to carry into milk.
- 'From all groups . . . adrenal to body weight percentages and adrenal to brain weight percentages of the right adrenal were significantly greater than those of the controls.' In other words, when compared with untreated animals the right adrenal gland of BST-treated animals was inflamed.
- 'The left adrenal absolute weight . . . for all treated groups was significantly increased.'
- 'The absolute kidney weights . . . were significantly greater than those of the control group.'
- 'The heart to body weight percentages for the three times and five times groups were considerably greater than those of the control group . . .'
- 'The liver to body weight percentages . . . were significantly increased.'
- 'Statistically significant weight increases also occurred for lung, pituitary and left ovary.'

The Monsanto files also indicated that BST levels in treated cows appeared in concentrations up to 1200 times higher than that of the natural BST in the blood of untreated cows.

These facts contradict the claims made by the chemical industries involved.

Yes, they do. The Chairman of the US Congressional Committee on Government Operations wrote to the Inspector General of the Department of Health and Human Services as follows:

> Specifically, I am seriously distressed with allegations concerning critical research information that has been withheld from public scrutiny by the Food and Drug Administration and the Monsanto Agricultural Company, in efforts to approve commercial use of Bovine Growth Hormone, without regard to the adverse health effects on animals and humans. More importantly, and contrary to the public assurances made by both the Food and Drug Administration and Monsanto, the industry files indicate high levels of the hormone are found in the milk of cows treated with synthetic Bovine Growth Hormones . . . Further, I am deeply concerned that little actual research exists on the human safety aspects of Bovine Growth Hormone.[24]

But on 5 November 1993, under pressure from the agrochemical lobby, the Food and Drug Administration yielded, notwithstanding the protest of the

General Accounting Office, another branch of the
US administration, as well as the official in charge
of consumer protection in the State of New York
who both stressed the risk to public health.

No doubt to protect itself from litigation, Monsanto itself has now published the following information about BST:

Use of POSILAC may result in reduced pregnancy
rates in injected cows and an increase in days open
for first calf heifers. Use of POSILAC has also
been associated with increases in cystic ovaries and
disorders of the uterus during the treatment
period. Cows injected with POSILAC may have
small decreases in gestation length and birth
weight of calves and they may have increased
twinning rates. Also, the incidence of retained
placenta may be higher following subsequent
calving . . .

Cows injected with POSILAC are at an
increased risk for clinical mastitis (visibly abnormal
milk). The number of cows with clinical mastitis
and the number of cases per cow may increase. In
addition, the risk of subclinical mastitis (milk not
visibly abnormal) is increased. In some herds, use
of POSILAC has been associated with increases in
somatic cell counts . . .

Use of POSILAC may result in an increase in

digestive disorders such as indigestion, bloat, and
diarrhoea . . .

Studies indicated that cows injected with POSI-
LAC had increased numbers of enlarged hocks and
lesions (e.g. lacerations, enlargements, calluses) of
the knee (carpal region), and second lactation or
older cows had more disorders of the foot region.[25]

The public reaction to the government approval
of BST was immediate. Numerous retail food
chains and milk distribution chains refused to sell
the polluted product. Monsanto's response was to
sue several small dairy concerns which informed
consumers that their milk was BST-free and
printed this on their label.

Monsanto's decision to sue indicates the lengths
to which the company was willing to go to force
BST onto the market. It has also come to light that
Monsanto has applied considerable political pressure to avoid an official study on the consequences
to society of using BST.[26] In August 1994, the US
Justice Department was petitioned to launch an
investigation.

For their part, the European authorities have
focused their attention on whether BST is needed
at all during a time of surplus milk production, and
whether large supplies of cheap, hormone-induced

milk would drive small farmers out of business. In July 1993 the European Commission recommended a seven-year ban on BST, an action which was ratified by the European Parliament. In December the Parliament went further, voting to dissociate the ban on BST from the issue of milk quotas (paving the way for a total ban, irrespective of EU milk production levels) and to extend it to milk and milk products from BST-treated cows imported from other countries. Almost simultaneously, however, the Council of Ministers decided to ignore both the European Commission and the European Parliament and to reduce the moratorium from seven years to one. BST milk might be on sale in Europe as early as 1995.

As David Martin MEP, a vice-president of the European Parliament, commented, 'It is a constitutional outrage that the Council of Ministers should act in this fashion. Meeting in secret, it is probably acting on the advice of top-level government advisers with vested industrial interests.'[27]

Britain and Belgium are thought to have pushed for immediate abandonment of the moratorium. Gillian Shephard, then British Agriculture Minister, claimed that licensing BST would 'avoid international trading problems'[28] – in other words, that under GATT any European ban on BST, however temporary, could be illegal as an impediment to free trade and that for this reason the drug should be marketed in Europe. Here is another example of the doctrine of free trade taking precedence over the most fundamental need of society, public health. And it illustrates the complicity that has developed between politicians and business interests.

Further evidence of this complicity is provided by a memo to the House of Commons European Select Committee from the Ministry of Agriculture. The Ministry cites Dista Products at Speke in Merseyside to make its point: 'Investment of 40 million pounds could be affected, together with 150 jobs. The [European] Commission communication [i.e. the seven-year moratorium] means that a considerable domestic and EC export market would continue to be unavailable for these products', and a BST ban would 'pose a serious threat to the development and commercialization of bio-technology . . . and deter investment'.[29] It seems that at no time do the governing elites concern themselves with the jobs lost in rural communities as a result of intensive agriculture – which are by nature less obviously quantifiable than industrial jobs – nor with the potentially serious effects on public health.

THE TRAP

Must one conclude that biotechnology should be rejected entirely?

No. In human medicine, as a means of curing specific diseases, biotechnology will be useful but we must exercise particularly tight controls over its development so as to avoid serious accidents. In agriculture, I feel that the disadvantages greatly outweigh the advantages. Let's take the case of the most extraordinary form of biotechnology: genetic engineering, also known as recombinant DNA technology. The aim of genetic engineering is to transfer genes from one cell to another and thereby to create new forms of life. It is now possible to manipulate and transfer genes from one species to another. For example, researchers at the University of Kentucky have transferred genes from a fish to a soya bean plant.[30] Other researchers have introduced a gene for the human growth hormone into a pig.[31]

In agriculture genetic engineering is applied to plants, animals, bacteria and viruses. The consequences of genetically altering the plant realm are far-reaching. Supporters of biotechnology claim that genetically engineered seeds will produce crops which are tolerant of herbicides and more resistant to drought, frosts, disease and pests. It is also claimed that they will reduce the need for chemical fertilizers and insecticides.

As a result of lobbying by the biotechnology industry, it is now possible to obtain a patent on living organisms altered by genetic engineering. New life forms will become patented commercial monopolies.

Of course, there are those who consider this new industry to be unacceptably dangerous. Debate must be encouraged, as we are playing with the fundamental elements of all life on earth.

The principal arguments against genetically engineered seeds are:

One: This is a perilous replay of the Green Revolution which attempted to transform agricultural processes by advanced scientific methods during the 1950s and 1960s. At the time there was great enthusiasm for synthetic organic chemicals. Natural raw materials were replaced and yields increased by applying chemicals to genetically selected strains of seeds which became known as 'miracle strains'. This led to the development of monocultures; in other words, it converted large areas to be used for growing a single crop of similar genetic origin. It also resulted in greater mechanization and ever-increasing use of chemicals and energy. As Fowler and Mooney, laureates of the Right Livelihood Award (known as the Alternative

Nobel Prize), put it, 'achieving high yield required fertilizer and irrigation. Fertilizer and irrigation nourished weeds as well as crops, creating the need for herbicides. And pests found the uniformity of new varieties appetizing which necessitated the use of insecticides as well . . . The fertilizers made the new varieties possible. The new varieties made the fertilizer necessary.'[32]

Two: Contrary to the industry's claims, the use of herbicide-tolerant seeds is likely to result in a need for more and stronger herbicides.

Recent studies at the University of California have demonstrated that pollen can be carried to plants over 1000 metres away and alter their genes. Thus, in the words of Dr David Ehrenfeld of Rutgers University: 'It will only be a few growing seasons before we can expect to see this engineered herbicide resistance transferred naturally, in the field, to the weeds themselves.'[33]

Three: The way of the world is constant change, evolution and adaptation. Insects develop resistance to insecticides just as weeds develop resistance to herbicides. In the US, despite a tenfold increase in the use of insecticides, annual crop losses to insects over the years have nearly doubled.[34]

Similarly, the agents that cause diseases evolve and can adapt to new circumstances. In a relatively short time, mutations will enable them to break through the defences of the genetically engineered plants and as they are genetically homogeneous – in other words, all vulnerable to the same diseases – whole crops could be eliminated.

Scientists cannot predict reliably how the new altered organisms will evolve and behave once released.

Four: It will never be possible to control the releases into the environment of untested and unauthorized organisms. Since 1986, numerous examples of such behaviour have come to light.[35]

Five: The development of genetically engineered monocultures will cause further devastation of the world's genetic resources. Genetic diversity is one of nature's greatest treasures. Many years ago the plant pathologist Martin Wolfe, working with the geneticist John Barrett, confirmed that poly-cultures are healthier than monocultures.[36] They demonstrated that a blend of three different types of barley was almost entirely resistant to mildew, whereas the three when grown separately were not. Should an infection attack one particular variety, each stem, surrounded by other varieties, is shielded by its resistant neighbours which them-selves might not be affected. They concluded that whereas a monoculture might produce higher yields in a given year, the polyculture produces more over the long term.

THE TRAP

What would be the dangers resulting from the loss of genetic diversity?

History supplies many well-known warnings. For example, there are still 5000 varieties of potato grown around the world. But in Ireland in the nineteenth century, all potatoes descended from only two varieties. The genetic limitation resulted in a lack of resistance to potato blight, which therefore reached epidemic proportions and caused the great famine.[37]

After the Southern corn leaf blight of the 1960s, the US National Academy of Science confirmed that the principal cause of the epidemic was corn crop uniformity. The corn variety in use was based on a hybrid. The Academy concluded: 'When one genetic component became susceptible to the new blight, the whole American crop became vulnerable.'[38]

The same is true of the Russian wheat epidemic of the 1970s. Forty million hectares had been sown with a single variety of a so-called 'miracle strain'. Unexpectedly and despite scientific experimentation, the strain sometimes proved incapable of surviving the harsh winter. Because of genetic uniformity, the consequence was a general crop failure.[39]

Intensive agriculture destroys genetic diversity

not only in seeds, but also, of course, in all forms of animal and vegetable life subjected to cloning, embryo transfer, gene selection, creation of mono-cultures, tissue culture, genetic engineering and the other processes of intensive agriculture. The granting of patents for new life forms will acceler-ate this trend because patent law requires that the new varieties be internally consistent, that is to say uniform. Also, new varieties will have to be genet-ically uniform to be registered with the appropriate authorities, and it will be illegal to sell unregistered seed.

As farmers must survive in a competitive world, they will farm intensively or be driven out of business. What is more, farmers will become tied to and dependent on the chemical suppliers. As the patented seeds and their plants will be geneti-cally engineered to respond to particular chemicals, the suppliers of those chemicals will control the farmers who use the seeds.

What are the questions that should be asked and answered before we proceed too far with biotechnology?

Can we understand the long-term effects, direct and indirect, of these wholly new and partially explored products? Can we obtain their benefits without terrible consequences? Do we really believe that new regulations will be sufficient to stop uncontrolled releases into the biosphere of these new forms of life? How can we prevent new forms of life, such as genetically engineered microbes, causing unlimited damage? Their very 'newness' means that existing life on earth, both animal and vegetable, has never been exposed to them and therefore has no immunity against them. Do we understand that by creating instantaneous, unexplored new forms of life we have thrown away the vital protection of being able to learn from our mistakes?

With thousands of researchers experimenting throughout the world and using their imaginations to create instantaneous new life forms unknown to nature and therefore untested by the trial and error of millions of years of natural evolution, is it possible to avoid mistakes and accidents which could have unimaginable consequences? We should always remember that there are no reliable shortcuts for testing new chemicals. Their effects may take years to become apparent.

But there are deeper questions. Has man the moral right to create new microbes, new animals, new life forms? Are we wise to transform the course of evolution artificially and to do so instantaneously? Do we realize that much of the change is irreversible? Can we convert animals and fields and forests and all things living into unnatural high-performing machines whose only purpose is to serve human beings? Is changing fundamental genetic information in living things, which will remain an inherited characteristic, the ultimate form of pollution?

Has the hubris of mankind become dangerously inflamed?

What solutions do you propose?

We need to revise our priorities. The purpose of agriculture is not just to produce the maximum amount of food, at the cheapest direct cost, employing the least number of people. The true purpose should be to produce a diversity of food, of a quality which respects human health, in a way which cares for the environment and which aims at maintaining employment at a level that ensures social stability in rural communities.

That means transforming the ways in which many developed nations subsidize their farmers and their agriculture?

Yes. Most official support, including that traditionally provided by Europe's Common Agricultural Policy, is granted on the basis that the state will buy a farmer's production at a fixed price. If a system is based on quantity, the natural consequence is that farmers will want to produce the maximum amount and intensify their methods of production.

Are you suggesting moving to organic farming and, if so, can it be economic?

I am not suggesting a general move to organic farming. I *am* suggesting a return to a form of agriculture that substantially reduces the use of pesticides, chemical fertilizers, pharmaceuticals such as hormones and antibiotics, and the products of biotechnology. Many analyses of farms operated in this manner have been done. David Pimentel of the New York State College of Agriculture and Life Sciences at Cornell University has shown that less intensive methods can produce food economically.[40] The trouble, of course, is that unsound and destructive agriculture makes a quicker profit in the short term than sound and healthy agriculture. Obviously, the quick profit only appears if indirect costs are not taken into account.

I have already quoted the studies of Herman Daly and John Cobb which indicate that when productivity is measured in terms of production per acre, or of energy consumed or capital invested, smaller farms show greater productivity. The large, mechanized modern monocultures come out best when productivity is measured in terms of numbers of people employed.

Who would be the losers and who would be the winners if we moved from intensive to less intensive methods of agriculture?

Let's start with the winners. The stability of rural communities would be re-established. The cities and their inhabitants would benefit as the exodus from the countryside ceases. Consumers would have healthy food to eat. Pollution of the environment by chemical and biotechnological products would be substantially reduced. Nations throughout the world would be relieved of the cost of welfare which has to be paid to those who are uprooted from the land and find no employment. Nor would they have to invest in further urban infrastructure to receive rural refugees.

The losers are easy to identify: the chemical and the biotechnology industries, along with their paid experts and lobbyists.

6

Nuclear Energy: The Big Lie

You believe that it is possible to make a very major change in our energy policy?

Yes. Technology is now available which would allow us to transform the way we produce and use energy. If we seize the opportunity to make a radical change, the effects would be extraordinarily beneficial to the economy, the environment and public safety.

What has suddenly changed to make you so optimistic?

The Cold War has ended. During the Cold War, the principal weapons were nuclear. Nuclear energy was an extension of military research and both were to some degree controlled by the same state scientific elites, which for reasons of national security maintained secrecy even when the nuclear programme was extended to non-military projects. Successive governments believed that if problems arose in the civil project, these should be kept secret so as not to endanger the military programme.

At first it was thought that nuclear energy would be safe and unlimited, and therefore would put an end to western dependence on imported energy. It was also believed that electricity generated by nuclear means would be, as the Chairman of the US Atomic Energy Commission declared, 'too cheap to meter'.[1] Western governments devoted a major part of their resources to developing nuclear energy. Between 1979 and 1990 the member nations of the International Energy Agency spent nearly 60 per cent of their energy research budget on nuclear power. Only 9.4 per cent was devoted to developing renewable sources of energy and 6.4 per cent to methods for saving energy.[2]

With almost unlimited state backing, nuclear scientists and administrators operated in secret and above the law. These 'nucleocrats' formed a sort of state within the state. Even when it became obvious that nuclear energy was both uneconomic and extremely dangerous, the facts were hidden from the public.

Now, with the end of the Cold War, this could change.

What are the alternatives that we should consider?

The technologies needed to transform the use of energy already exist and are commercially available. The USA is leading the field.

In America, energy is consumed in three main sectors of activity: residential and commercial demand, which accounts for 36 per cent of energy use; industrial activity, which accounts for 37 per cent; and transport, which accounts for 27 per cent.[3] It is now possible to reduce very substantially the energy consumed in all these sectors while providing unchanged or better services. The benefits would be numerous. First, economic growth would be de-coupled from energy consumption. At the moment, the conventional wisdom is that the use of energy increases in lockstep with the growth of the economy. That would no longer be true. In fact, we could dramatically reduce energy consumption per unit of output with corresponding financial savings. Second, the impact on the environment, including on global warming, would be similarly reduced. Third, dependence on imported energy could be progressively minimized or eliminated. Finally, new industries based on these new technologies would be a source of healthy economic growth.

What opportunities exist to improve our use of electricity?

The North American utilities' think tank, the Electric Power Research Institute, estimates that the full use of new technology could reduce the consumption of electricity in the USA, through cost-effective means, by as much as 55 per cent.[4]

The US Department of Energy and the Environmental Protection Agency believe that as much as 80 per cent of the electricity now used for lighting could be saved by technological improvements.[5]

Rocky Mountain Institute estimates that 75 per cent of the electricity now consumed in houses, offices and factories in the United States could be saved by installing existing technology. This technology is cost-effective and would not reduce – indeed, would often improve – the quality of service.[6]

The largest US investor-owned utility, Pacific Gas and Electric Company, expects to satisfy 75 per cent of its new requirements for power in the present decade by increasing customer efficiency, and therefore reducing need. The remainder would be drawn from renewable sources of energy. The group expects never to have to build a new generating station and it has dissolved its civil engineering and construction division. As recently as 1981 it was planning to build ten major new generating stations.

How can we obtain these savings?

Rocky Mountain Institute has published documentation on electric efficiency which is extremely comprehensive, and which includes a multitude of examples.[7] For instance, Southwire, the largest independent wire and cable manufacturer in the USA, has reduced its consumption of electricity and gas by 40 per cent and 60 per cent respectively, per kilogram of production. The large Compaq Computer Corporation has already cut its electricity use by 50 per cent in its offices in Houston, Texas. Douglas Emmett, a property development company, has reduced electricity consumption in an office building in California by 75 per cent. Pacific Gas and Electric Company has achieved a similar reduction in its old office building in San Ramon, California, and in a new one in Antioch, California. What is more, they have recently completed an experimental house in Davis, California, where summer temperatures can reach 45 degrees centigrade. This ordinary-looking, mid-priced tract house needs neither heating nor cooling equipment and is expected to use only one-fifth of the energy prescribed by the strictest US building standards.

If its innovations were widely practised, it would cost about $1,800 *less* to build than a normal similar house.

The technologies used are numerous. They include new insulation methods; windows which admit light but which insulate from heat; lighting systems which while improving visibility reduce electricity consumption by 80 to 90 per cent; new air-conditioning systems which reduce the consumption of electricity per unit of cooling by more than 90 per cent; and so on.[8]

The capital investment required if the US as a whole were to move over to these new systems has been estimated at about 200 billion dollars. The annual saving would be in the order of 100 to 130 billion dollars, a spectacular rate of return.[9]

Do the same opportunities exist in Europe?

The US has traditionally used more energy relative to its GNP than has Europe, principally because energy in the US has been cheap. But opportunities for vast savings also exist in Europe. Detailed studies have shown that it would be possible to save 50 per cent of electricity consumption in Sweden and up to 75 per cent of electricity used in buildings in Denmark. In Germany it may be possible to save up to 80 per cent of electricity consumed by private households. All these savings were shown to be highly cost-effective.[10]

What about transport?

About two-thirds of the gasoline consumed in the US is used in transport. Technology already exists which would allow a 50 per cent efficiency improvement in the performance of light vehicles, and the Big Three US auto manufacturers have agreed with the US government to develop tripled-efficiency models.

Dr A. B. Lovins of Rocky Mountain Institute considers that the next, imminent, technological revolution will bring us what he calls the 'ultra-light hybrid-electric supercar'. In a recent study Lovins describes how an ultralight vehicle for five passengers will be able to travel 100 kilometres using less than 1.6 litres of gasoline or other fuel. He claims that the vehicle will be safer, more durable, quieter and more comfortable than existing vehicles, yet will be no more expensive. According to Lovins, the progress that has been made in the fields of aerodynamics, polymer-composite ultralight materials, microelectronics, power electronics, advanced motor and energy storage technologies, computer-aided design and manufacturing and advanced software could reduce fuel consumption dramatically. Similar improvements are available in heavy vehicles. Together, they could reduce by five-sixths the consumption of gasoline by vehicles in the United States. Worldwide, they could save as much oil as OPEC now extracts.[11] This would also massively reduce the damage done to the environment by gasoline and diesel emissions.

How likely are we to see these new technologies put into practice?

In America changes are happening fast. Europe too can participate in this great revolution – except for those countries which are held back by the immense power of the nucleocrats. They are fighting for the survival of their industry and do so by disseminating false information about its cost and its safety. With state backing, they make wholly untrue claims in their propaganda and they do their best to cover up every dangerous incident that occurs. If we allow ourselves to be dominated by this powerful bureaucracy, then our nations' economies will be paralyzed by an aging nuclear industry. Countries such as France will become museums of obsolete technology.

THE TRAP

What new sources of energy are coming into use in the US?

All of our present principal sources of energy – oil, coal and gas – damage the environment, and of course nuclear power is particularly dangerous. Combined heat and power technologies used in conjunction with conventional fossil fuels – especially natural gas, a relatively clean resource known to be abundant – will play a useful transitional role, given their economic viability and environmental benefits. (In a combined heat and power station the hot steam and water produced during the generation of electricity are reused to provide space or water heating rather than being wasted. Similar 'cogeneration' can provide valuable high-temperature heat for industry as a by-product of making electricity. Such practices roughly double the efficiency with which the energy stored in the fuel is used.)

However, the long-term solution, besides reducing energy needs sevenfold through more efficient use, is to develop the sustainable and clean sources of energy which in the past have been starved of research investment because attention has been concentrated principally on nuclear power. In the US, as in some European countries, progress has been made in the use of geothermal, wind and solar power. Together with biomass they now produce 11 per cent of California's electricity and cause virtually no air pollution.[12] All renewable sources now produce at least 8 per cent (unofficial estimates are higher) of total US energy, and have provided roughly a third of the net increase in US energy supply since 1979.[13]

Geothermal energy originates in the earth's crust, like the power beneath volcanoes. World-wide geothermal generating capacity is growing fast. It provides 28 per cent of the power in Nicaragua, 26 per cent in the Philippines, and 9 per cent in Kenya.[14] The US Department of the Environment estimates that hydrothermal reservoirs, which are hot water and vapour systems trapped underground, are in theory able to provide thirty times as much energy as is currently used in the US.[15]

Wind is another growing source of power. Twenty thousand turbines have been installed throughout the world. The breakthrough allowing the use of wind power followed technological improvements such as advanced blades, improved transmission and generators, and larger turbines, all of which have reduced costs to about 6 cents per kilowatt-hour (the latest California competitive bids, unsubsidized, are 4.5 to 4.8 cents per kilowatt-hour).[16] Drs Michael Grubb and Niels

Meyer, in their important study on wind energy, explain how wind power can become a substantial source of energy in America, where it now provides enough power to run San Francisco, and worldwide.[17]

Solar energy is the most important source of all. Large-scale solar thermal power plants promise to become highly economic producers. They receive and concentrate the sun's rays to heat liquids, producing steam for a turbine which in turn generates electricity. Already costs have fallen from 26 cents per kilowatt-hour in 1984 to about 8 or 9 cents now.[18] As the example of the Davis house demonstrates, passive solar technology on a smaller and more individual scale is also a development with considerable potential. And tens of thousands of US buildings already obtain most or all of their electricity from photovoltaics (solar cells), now becoming competitive in many applications. Pacific Gas and Electric Company found, for example, that photovoltaics are cost-effective *today* for supporting a fully-loaded substation, and the Sacramento Municipal Utility District finds it cheaper to power alley lights with solar electricity than to connect to the power systems of adjacent buildings. Such advantages are rapidly spreading solar cells worldwide. A comprehensive US government study found in 1990 that combining these and other commercially successful renewable resources could cost-effectively meet most or all US needs for electricity and for total energy in 2030, about the retirement date of a conventional power plant ordered today.[19]

Nuclear was thought to be the energy source of the future. What are the arguments against it?

Let's start with the British experience. In 1988, the Thatcher government decided to privatize the electricity generating industry, including nuclear power.

Obviously, if it is to be sold to the public, an industry must give promise of a profitable future. The Thatcher government sincerely believed that this was the case with nuclear energy. The British nucleocracy had provided assurances and backed them with a multitude of figures. But it is a normal legal requirement that prior to privatization a full prospectus must be published which describes the industry, its results and its potential. The prospectus is prepared by independent investment bankers using independent accountants. Thus, the real facts started to emerge.

For example, on 5 July 1988 it was disclosed that the industry was proposing to change its accounting rules. Quite simply, it planned to prolong to 135 years the date by which nuclear power stations would be fully decommissioned and returned to green-field sites.[20] This accountancy trick made it possible to depreciate the power stations over a longer period and thereby artificially embellish the accounts.

On 27 July 1988, the Energy Select Committee of the House of Commons submitted its report stating: 'We are concerned about the costs of nuclear power . . . We are disturbed by the uneven treatment given to coal and nuclear by the Government; the problems of nuclear have been glossed over while there has been an emotional hostility towards the coal industry.'[21] This is an important comment. The development of British nuclear energy was substantially influenced by the political desire to destroy the National Union of Mineworkers, which had been led by a Marxist and had brought down Edward Heath's Conservative government.

In December 1988, the government published its Electricity Bill. The Bill included a suggestion that the government grant a subsidy to the nuclear industry so as to make it appear profitable. In July 1989, the then Secretary of State for Energy announced to the House of Commons: 'As a result of our preparations for privatization, it has become clear that the cost of reprocessing and waste treatment of spent Magnox nuclear fuel will be a great deal higher than has been charged in electricity prices and provided for in the accounts of the Central Electricity Generating Board and the South of Scotland Electricity Board . . . It has been decided that both the assets and liabilities relating to the Magnox stations . . . should remain under Government control. The advanced gas-cooled reactor stations will . . . [however] be privatized.'[22]

On 31 October 1989 the *Financial Times* business bulletin *Power In Europe* published a leaked Cabinet document which confirmed that the cost of nuclear energy is roughly double that of energy generated by conventional means.[23]

On 9 November 1989, the Minister of Energy announced to the House of Commons that the whole project of privatizing the nuclear industry, including the gas-cooled reactors, would be withdrawn. He also announced a five-year moratorium on the construction of nuclear power stations. On the same day in the House of Commons the Secretary of State for Scotland explained that neither the government's own experts nor its financial advisers were able to establish the cost of decommissioning existing power stations.

Nigel Lawson, then the Chancellor of the Exchequer and a former Minister of Energy, describes the privatization process thus:

Another important area where the received wisdom was eventually shown to be seriously flawed . . . was nuclear power . . . It turned out that for years the Central Electricity Generating Board, wittingly or unwittingly, had been making a deceptive case in favour of the economics of nuclear power . . . the CEGB had been under-providing for, and greatly understating the likely true cost of, decommissioning a nuclear power station at the end of its life. They had been able to get away with this because no nuclear power station had so far been decommissioned . . . Had it not been for privatization, who knows how much longer the country would have been paying the price of the phoney economics of nuclear power.[24]

How did the British nucleocrats react to this?

For a few years they kept a low profile. But now they are regaining confidence. Nuclear Electric has recently appointed a research company to advise it in choosing a new name. The list of fifteen titles to be considered includes the names Safeco, Enviro-gen, GenCo and Britannia Electric, but nothing suggesting nuclear power.[25]

But the facts which continue to emerge demonstrate how far the nucleocracy went to produce misleading figures and to conceal the truth. In

1988 the Central Electricity Generating Board estimated the costs to a privatized nuclear operator of dealing with spent fuel and waste plus decommissioning liabilities at 2.63 billion pounds. In 1989 the figure rose to 7.63 billion pounds.[26] In 1987 British Nuclear Fuels estimated the cost of decommissioning its contaminated plants at 438 million pounds. In 1988 this figure was raised to 4.6 billion pounds.[27]

In 1989, when the British attempt to privatize nuclear energy was abandoned, the decommissioning costs were forecast to reach 15 billion pounds. The latest estimates suggest that the total undiscounted cost of decommissioning the UK's existing nuclear installations has reached 22 to 23 billion pounds.[28]

These figures provide some indication of the financial burden future generations will be forced to carry as a result of the short-sightedness and deviousness of the nucleocrats.

Are there similar cases elsewhere?

In the US the nuclear industry was forced by the courts to disclose a fair number of its secrets about safety, reliability, economics and other awkward issues. The result has been that all nuclear power plants ordered since 1973 have subsequently been cancelled and no new orders have been placed since 1978. The main causes for cancellation were safety, the growing costs of construction and maintenance (which had already reached three to five times the level originally predicted), and the existence of rules passed by forty-three states which require public utilities to meet electric services in the least costly way possible. Once the facts became known, nuclear power stations were unable to satisfy these requirements. Indeed, an authoritative analysis found that by the end of the 1990s, at least one-third of the US nuclear plants now in operation are likely to be permanently closed and uneconomic to operate. And most US utilities agree that it is cheaper to build, fuel and operate (for the next thirty years) a combined cycle gas-fired power plant than merely to fuel and maintain a typical US nuclear power plant.[29]

Nuclear energy has no future except where energy production is centrally planned, where economically competitive options are suppressed, and where no open and informed democratic debate is possible. Wherever nuclear energy has been subjected to the test of the free market, it has not survived. The conditions for the survival of nuclear energy, therefore, are state subsidies and an absence of free debate.

France is generally considered to have succeeded in building an effective nuclear industry, which is thought to be both economic and safe. Is that the case?

No. That some people believe it to be true is merely testimony to the effectiveness of the nucleocrats' propaganda campaigns.

Nuclear power stations generate 78 per cent of France's electricity at a price generally thought to be competitive. But it is vital to understand the difference between price and cost. The price is the figure at which the industry sells electricity to consumers. The cost is the actual money spent by the industry in producing the electricity. The price can be lower than the cost because of enormous subsidies, both direct and indirect, from the state as well as cross-subsidies from other activities of Electricité de France, the public utility which supplies electricity. Of course, as in England, the cost should include the amounts needed to decommission obsolete nuclear power stations and to store radioactive waste. This is practically imposs-ible to calculate because we don't know how to fully decommission obsolete plants, how to dispose of radioactive waste, or even how to store it safely for the long term. Even Electricité de France implicitly admits this to be the case in its reply to the French government auditing office where it states that the future cost of decommissioning 'continues to be provided for on the basis of old estimates, in the absence of more reliable figures'.[30]

Despite this disparity between price and cost, and despite the claims of the nucleocrats, electricity prices in France are not low.

The German Electricity Generating Companies Federation published the prices of electricity charged throughout Europe during 1992.[31] The study referred to residential use based on an average annual consumption of 3500 kilowatt-hours. French prices were higher than those of the Netherlands, Denmark, Ireland, Luxembourg, Germany, Greece and Great Britain. Of those countries, Denmark, Ireland, Luxembourg and Greece use no nuclear power. The Netherlands generates only 2 per cent of its electricity from nuclear power; and even the highest users, Germany and Great Britain (34 per cent and 27.2 per cent respectively) come in at less than half of France's figure of 78 per cent.[32]

The French Ministry of Industry's figures for 1993 show that despite using assumptions which are particularly favourable to nuclear energy, electricity generated by nuclear means is 50 per cent more expensive than electricity produced by combined heat and power plants using coal-fired steam turbines. If gas turbines are used, electricity generated by nuclear means remains more expensive; and it is only marginally cheaper than that generated by wind turbines placed in suitable locations.[33]

What is most significant is the way Electricité de France handles these facts. In an internal report dated June 1989 concerning commercial strategy for the years 1990 through 1992, the company describes combined heat and power and the decentralized production of electricity as 'threats'. It recommends the need to oppose combined heat and power by 'exercising pressure on the public authorities'.[34]

Let me tell you an anecdote. When this book was first published in French, it gave rise to considerable debate. As a result I was invited to discuss it at a meeting of about forty Establishment industrialists. During the meeting, not unexpectedly, I was severely attacked by a leading nucleocrat. After an exchange of ideas, the floor was taken by a major industrialist who had been one of the fathers of the French nuclear programme. He reminded us that he had been a member of the committee which had first established France's nuclear strategy and announced that he had come to the meeting to perform what he called his 'act of contrition'. With hindsight, he said, the decisions taken by the committee had been wrong on grounds both of economic viability and of safety. A great quiet descended on the meeting.

What about the safety record of the nuclear energy industry?

The history of the nuclear energy industry can be summed up as a long succession of dissimulations and lies. Of course, the best known example is Chernobyl.

In the aftermath of the accident, Alexander Lutsko, who is now Rector of the International Sakharov College of Radioecology, described the attitudes of the nucleocrats at the International Atomic Energy Agency: 'Samples of soil and food-stuffs supplied for the purpose of measuring radio-activity suddenly were placed under lock and key. After consultations, the International Atomic Energy Agency asked me not to demand the handing over of the test results because the Agency did not wish to become involved in their possible use for political ends.'[35]

Alla Yarochinskaya, a deputy of the Supreme Soviet and a member of various committees of inquiry on Chernobyl, has published a book entitled *Chernobyl: The Forbidden Truth*. Her conclusion: 'The lies about Chernobyl are as terrifying as the catastrophe itself.'[36]

Following the Chernobyl disaster, the Minister of the Environment of Saar province in Germany declared in the Bundestag: 'Attitudes to the safety of nuclear reactors and the provision of information in France are also a great cause for concern. On 9 May 1986, the French Embassy in Bonn issued this statement: "By reason of its remoteness from Chernobyl, French territory has not been affected by radioactive emissions."' The Minister of the Environment went on to say, 'This was a week and a half after we had taken measurements showing concentrations two thousand times higher than normal in Saarland and in Rhineland-Palatinate. While we were warning people not to consume fresh milk and vegetables, the French authorities were completely silent. Silent, and the population was kept in the dark. The culture of secrecy in France is as hostile to man as is censorship in the Soviet Union.'[37]

Where does the truth lie?

No one knows the full extent of the truth. We can only glimpse some of the exposed parts of the iceberg. The then President of the Ukraine, Leonid Kravchuk, declared at the World Economic Forum in Davos in Switzerland that 11 million people had been affected by the Chernobyl accident.[38] Others involved have also made some revelations. Here are a few of them:

- Leonid Ichtchenko, Chief Medical Officer of the Narodichi district hospital: 'We have examined all the children in the district several times. 80 per cent of them suffer from thyroid hypertrophy.'[39]
- Alexander Satchko, Director of the Narodichi District Polyclinic: 'All 5,000 children in the district have been irradiated by iodine 131.'[40]
- The Ukrainian periodical *Kiewske Wedomosti* stated that in the single district of Kharkov 3633 people were said to have been irradiated.[41]
- In September 1992, the World Health Organization (WHO) announced that in Belarus the number of cases of thyroid cancer in children had multiplied twenty-four-fold. Dr Wilfried Kreisel, coordinator of the WHO's International Programme on the Health Effects of the Chernobyl Accident, declared, 'We are absolutely clear this increase after the accident is a result of the accident.'[42] Two years later, the thyroid cancer rate among Ukrainian children has increased sixty-two-fold.[43]
- According to the Chernobyl Committee of the Russian government, of those who took part in the clean-up of the Chernobyl site, 7,000 died during the seven years following the disaster.[44]
- In Norway, a study of 35,263 pregnancies and

23,880 births shows an increase of 13.5 per cent in miscarriages during the year following the explosion.[45]

One could continue quoting for a long time.

In the light of this evidence it is scandalous that the International Atomic Energy Agency failed to organize and publish a proper study of the consequences of the accident.

The need to cover up was illustrated as recently as 24 May 1993, when the daily energy bulletin *Enerpresse* reported that Jean-Paul Lannegrace, chairman of the French Nuclear Energy Society, had stated: 'After all, there were only thirty-one deaths at Chernobyl.'[46] Mr Lannegrace is also Deputy Director of the nuclear fuel manufacturing division of Framatome, France's leading producer of equipment for the nuclear industry. The International Atomic Energy Agency, to its shame, still claims similar figures.

In August 1992, two doctors responsible for nuclear medicine at a leading hospital in Lille asserted in an interview given to the local newspaper, *Nord Eclair*, that there were no health problems among the children of Chernobyl. The interview was part of an article headlined 'Children of Chernobyl do not suffer radiation sickness'.[47]

It should never be forgotten that nuclear fallout produces effects of a special dimension. The deaths and serious diseases caused by a nuclear accident cannot be counted easily because they occur over a long period of time and do not carry a label specifically identifying their cause. As radioactive elements are carried by the winds and by water, their effects are geographically widespread. Contamination of the soil lasts for centuries. The principal isotope of plutonium has a half-life of 24,400 years.

And what is the state of Chernobyl today?

The Chernobyl site remains a terrible threat despite efforts to make it safe. In 1991, the number 2 reactor had to be closed because of a fire, and it has recently been discovered that the concrete sarcophagus surrounding the number 4 reactor (destroyed in the original disaster) is crumbling. It was built on wet cement. If it were to collapse, the radioactive debris released could be as much as in 1986.[48]

'Numerous safety deficiencies' exist in the operation of the two remaining nuclear reactors, according to an inspection team from the International Atomic Energy Agency.[49] These are caused not only by a shortage of money, but also by the fact that some 150 highly trained workers (about 20 per cent of the staff) have left following the breakdown of the USSR. Yet the Ukrainian authorities are unwilling to close the plant, as requested by international nuclear agencies. With Ukraine desperately short of both money and alternative sources of power, western governments are beginning to accept that they must provide support. To date they have agreed to supply some 800 million dollars, but there is significant disagreement as to how this money could best be spent.

The Ukrainian government says that it cannot close Chernobyl until it has completed the construction of five new VVER-1000 nuclear reactors, on which work was halted due to a lack of funds and to political reasons.[50] It finds support for its view, needless to say, from the West's nuclear companies, all of which anticipate rich pickings should construction recommence. However, major safety questions remain regarding the design of the VVER-1000. In 1993 the International Atomic Energy Agency found some sixteen areas in which the VVER-1000 design did not meet normal safety standards, including fire risk, embrittlement of pressurized steel vessels and containment of radioactive emissions.[51]

If the VVER-1000 plants are not completed, how else can Ukraine meet its energy requirements?

A much wiser solution would be to pursue the potential for energy efficiency identified by a recent US Department of Energy report,[52] the figures of which are agreed by the Ukrainian government. This reveals that the plan backed by the G7 countries (shutting down Chernobyl and opening the five VVER-1000s) is the most expensive option, and casts doubt on whether 800 million dollars would be sufficient even to close down the existing reactors at Chernobyl. By 1999, says the Energy Department, the five VVER-1000s would produce 5000 megawatts of electricity at a cost per kilowatt-hour of some 3 to 4 US cents. By the same date, basic improvements in industrial energy efficiency would save 4250 megawatts at a cost of only 1 to 2 cents for every kilowatt-hour saved. Speeding up existing plans for wind turbines and upgrading existing hydroelectric plants in Ukraine would produce an extra 2000 megawatts for between 2 and 3 cents per kilowatt-hour. Further improvements to Ukraine's fourteen coal-fired plants, it says, could produce an extra 2000 mega-watts 'at a much lower investment than would be required to build new generating capacity'. Ukraine currently needs five times more electricity for each unit of economic production than the OECD average.[53] An increase in energy efficiency, the use of renewable sources of energy and the use of combined heat and power plants would not only help solve the Chernobyl problem but would benefit the whole Ukrainian economy, creating valuable jobs in the process. The international nucleocracy is determined this should not happen.

But there is one leading nucleocrat who is moving in the right direction. Jean Syrota, chairman of the French nuclear group Cogema, admits that 'Chernobyl-type reactors can be shut down in a technically simple way. You just need to become more efficient in the use of electricity. Energy consumption in Eastern Europe has reached alarming levels because energy in these countries is almost free. If energy were priced realistically, its use would be better controlled and we would no longer need supplies from dangerous nuclear plants . . .'[54]

What should we do to help Russia and the Eastern European countries?

We must facilitate, by technical and financial means, the closure of their nuclear energy systems and their replacement by increased use of renewable sources of energy, enhanced efficiency in energy use, and combined heat and power plants using gas turbines. The turbines could be versions slightly adapted from those already manufactured for military aviation, an industry which needs to be converted to civilian uses. Natural gas supplies are abundant in Russia. Such power stations would not be costly, can be built rapidly and can be installed close to towns and factories needing their output.

But to do this, we must fight the western nucleocracy. As far as the nucleocrats are concerned, the failure of the nuclear industry in eastern countries could spell salvation for the nuclear industry in the West. If western nucleocrats can convince us that problems in the East only reflect communist incompetence, they will have found their goldmine. They will be able to re-equip the nuclear industry of the eastern countries, often at the expense of western taxpayers, and thereby revitalize their own industry. It is no accident that those western institutions which are responsible for solving energy problems in Russia and Eastern Europe are nearly all controlled by nucleocrats.

And what is the situation in Western Europe?

Western nucleocrats strive to make us believe that safety problems exist only in the east. In reality, there have been numerous instances in France and elsewhere. They are symptoms of the dangers inherent in the process itself, which are grave because their consequences can be so catastrophic. The most recent example in France was the fatal accident at the Cadarache reactor complex. An engineer was killed and four of his colleagues seriously injured while they tried to decommission a retired liquid sodium reactor. The blast, on 31 March 1994, brought down the concrete roof of an annex to the Rapsodie reactor, which contained 37 tonnes of sodium needing treatment.[55]

As long ago as 1990 Pierre Tanguy, Inspector-General of Electricité de France, wrote in his annual report: 'Today, the most worrying risk [in commercial light-water reactors used throughout the world] is that of a sudden break in one or more steam generator tubes.'[56] Steam generators are huge heat exchangers in a nuclear reactor, containing thousands of tubes through which the primary coolant circulates. A break in any one of these tubes can cause an accident through the loss of coolant, and a break in a handful of tubes can keep the emergency cooling systems from working. It can also lead to cooling water being emptied out of the reactor containment shell via safety valves. This can leave the core of the system uncovered and thereby trigger an accident of core meltdown, followed by a massive release of radioactivity. To date, throughout the world, eleven cases of ruptures in steam generator tubes have been reported.[57] It is possible that only a limited amount of radioactivity was released, but the state of steam generators has become an urgent issue. France has decided to replace the steam generators in twenty-four reactors, but so far work has been completed only on the Dampierre-1, Bugey-5 and Gravelines-1 reactors. Steam generators are also being replaced in Switzerland, Germany, Sweden and Belgium.

Another danger area is the vessel head. In September 1991 a leak was detected in the vessel head of the Bugey-3 reactor in France.[58] The cause was identified as a cracked penetration. These penetrations play a crucial role in the introduction of control rods into the reactor vessel. A break in one of them can lead to either or both of two accidents: an uncontainable loss of coolant, and significant damage to the shut-down system of the reactor which can lead to meltdown of the core.

By August 1993, nearly two years after this discovery, not even half of the potentially affected French reactors in operation had been fully checked. Of the twenty-four which had been inspected, some fifteen were found to have cracks.[59] The same failure has been identified on reactors in Sweden, Switzerland and Belgium.[60] What is more, in May 1993 circular cracks 18 mm in length and at least 4 mm deep were identified in Sweden's Ringhals-2 reactor.[61] This type of crack is particularly dangerous, because there is no leakage prior to a break and consequently the parts can rupture without warning.

There is another kind of problem. In May 1992, Electricité de France was officially informed that certain documents supplied by a contractor following work on the reactor at Dampierre-1 had been falsified. In fact two of the three welds involved were defective, and it transpired that the subcontractor had doctored the X-rays used for quality-control. Subsequently it was discovered that at least fifteen welds on three of the four reactors at Dampierre were defective.[62]

What will be the fate of existing nuclear power stations?

No large commercial nuclear power station which has been exposed to an intense neutron flux for many years, and hence is heavily contaminated, has ever been decommissioned or dismantled. Our knowledge of how to decommission such plants is limited as it has been applied to research reactors only and not to commercial reactors. In several of the examples I have given severe and unexpected metallurgical problems arose when thick sections of exotic steels and other alloys were exposed over a long period to a combination of intense radiation, heat, vibration and chemical corrosion.

Spare parts are the main source of future income for companies such as Framatome. Their commercial future looks prosperous, not as a result of the health of the industry, but because existing plants are forced to order spare parts on a much larger scale than was initially foreseen.

However, promising events are taking place. A very large electricity company in Canada, Ontario Hydro, has decided to close a substantial part of its nuclear capacity rather than undertake repairs. In the United States, old reactors such as those of the Yankee Rowe, Trojan and Rancho Seco stations are being closed down; additionally, work has begun to progressively close eleven other previously commercial plants.

Here again, of course, the endemic phenomenon of rapid cost escalations emerged. At Yankee Rowe, the estimated cost of 116.6 million dollars has risen to 247.1 million dollars. At Rancho Seco, the estimated cost has risen from 126.5 million dollars to 292.9 million dollars.[63]

On another subject, tell us about recent developments in the international trade in plutonium.

There are about 1000 tonnes of plutonium stockpiled around the world. Of this, 140 tonnes are highly suitable for making nuclear bombs, and the rest is perfectly usable.[64] Fifty-five years ago, there was none. Plutonium is man-made. A study by the Rand Corporation for the US Defense Department concludes that within a decade there will be enough plutonium in the world to manufacture 87,000 crude but formidable nuclear weapons.[65]

The original peaceful purpose for producing plutonium was to fuel fast breeder nuclear reactors. Even nucleocrats are being forced, reluctantly, to admit that fast breeders are dangerous and uneconomic. Some are being closed, such as the prototype fast reactor at Dounreay in Scotland and the Kalkar reactor in Germany. In France, Superphénix is being converted into an experimental centre. In reality that is no more than a face-saver for the French nucleocrats who fought to keep it open.

In Britain, the state-owned company British Nuclear Fuels built a thermal oxide reprocessing plant (THORP) at Sellafield in Cumbria. The purpose of the plant is to separate out plutonium and uranium from the spent fuel discharged from nuclear power stations in order to recycle the plutonium as fuel for fast breeder reactors. But with the closure or abandonment of fast breeders the market for plutonium has been very substantially reduced. On the other hand, the market for bombs to be sold to outlaws seems to be growing.

So why proceed with THORP?

It cannot be on economic grounds. The plant does not solve the problem of how to handle spent nuclear fuel; indeed, the volume of waste actually increases during reprocessing. Dry storage would be a better option than reprocessing and Scottish Nuclear has decided in future to dry-store its spent nuclear fuel rather than send it to THORP.[66] German utilities have calculated that they would save 3.5 billion Deutschmarks (over 2 billion dollars) by ceasing to have their spent fuel reprocessed at La Hague, the French equivalent of THORP, a decision taken on both economic and environmental grounds.[67]

THORP has further major disadvantages. First, its decommissioning costs will be at least 900 million pounds,[68] and some analysts believe much higher. Second, the plant will increase radioactive releases into both the sea and the air. The Irish Sea is already the most radioactively contaminated sea in the world[69] and consequently the Irish govern-

ment lobbied the British government not to open
THORP. Both the Committee on Medical Aspects
of Radiation in the Environment and the Department of Health were critical of the medical information provided by the government.[70] Finally,
THORP will contribute to the problem of plutonium proliferation.

The British government stood firm. It lacked the
guts to face the embarrassment of admitting that
THORP was a 2.8 billion pound white elephant,
and as a result the plant is now in operation.

7

Why?

During our conversations, you have described a number of fundamental problems facing modern society and have suggested some solutions. Why are we facing this crisis of civilization?

We have reached the end of an epoch. We need to understand where we are, what we have accomplished and where we seem to be heading. Many believe that the problems we face can be resolved by doing what we have always done, but doing it more effectively. They believe that we are going in the right direction but that we should redouble our efforts to achieve our objectives. Of them I ask three questions: how is it that nearly two hundred years after the birth of the Industrial Revolution, which produced humanity's greatest period of economic expansion, the absolute number of those living in misery, both material and social, has grown exponentially? How is it that the world's slum population has developed at a rate vastly greater than that of global population growth?[1] And how is it that despite incredible technological innovations the world now faces man-made threats of a quite different magnitude from the wars, famines, epidemics and other upheavals of previous dark ages?

Climate change threatens the stability of life; progressive destruction of the ozone layer could convert everyday sunlight into a mortal danger; both fresh and sea water are being poisoned; land and soil are being debased; the air in many areas is becoming dangerous to breathe; the food that we eat is polluted by toxic chemicals; and as United Nations Environmental Minister Maurice Strong said, we are living with the threat of 'up to forty potential Chernobyls waiting to happen', and that in Eastern Europe and the ex-Soviet Union alone.[2]

How is it that humanity's greatest leap forward in material prosperity has resulted in extreme social breakdown, and that our greatest period of technological and scientific achievement has come to endanger the conditions which allow life on earth? That is the extraordinary enigma which we must seek to understand.

What answers do you have to those questions?

To understand the behaviour and achievements of modern western society, we must start by studying its culture. Its religion, principally, is based on the premise that there is one God, the Creator, and that man is made in His image; that man and man alone is the personification of God on earth; that man is set apart from and is placed in a privileged position relative to all other forms of life. Nature, we believe, has been placed at man's disposal.

This is quite different from the religious outlook of primal peoples. They cannot conceive of man set apart from and unrelated to the animate and inanimate forces surrounding him. Men and women in these primal societies approach the natural world with care and reverence. In the primal world, man's relationship with nature is not one of exploitation, but one of harmony. In the modern western tradition, however, the natural world is something to be investigated, explained and ultimately used.

Buddhists and traditional Hindus, for their part, believe that the origin of the problems of our society lies in the dichotomy that we perceive between man and nature. They believe that the radical separation of man from nature follows from the fundamental premises of the Judeo-Christian tradition, and that within such a context nature is inevitably subjected to the will and aggressive instincts of man.

What are the convictions of the most recent of the great religions, Marxism-Leninism?

Marx and Lenin rejected spiritual values and placed their entire trust in science and technology. Marxism feels free to exploit nature, without limit, in the service of man.

Did not Enlightenment philosophers lay the ground for such thinking?

Of course. The principal beliefs of the Enlightenment were that human reason, freed from the impediments of tradition and prejudice, can and should emancipate man from the constraints of religion, history and the natural world. In other words, the Enlightenment sought to establish a morality detached from spiritual considerations and based exclusively on the rational. This, it was believed, would allow mankind to be liberated from everything that was impeding its progress.

This combination of faith in reason with humanist hubris, on which the Enlightenment was based, is the origin of the distinctive world view of modernism which inevitably led to Marxism. All the key Enlightenment ideas – the humanist elevation of mankind, the enthronement of scientific reason, the project of a universal civilization, the

liberation of humankind from all species of religion
– are expressed uncompromisingly in Marx's
thought. In fact, his ideas form a great synthesis of
Enlightenment themes, and that is one reason why
they were able to cast a spell over western
intellectuals.

*How would you define the rational within this
context?*

The rational was identified with science, and
science was seen as the instrument with which
humans could master nature. René Descartes, the
pivotal philosopher of modernity, states that men
should be 'the masters and possessors of nature'[3]
and he considered science to be the necessary tool.
Francis Bacon, the English Enlightenment thinker,
held that facts established in a scientific way have
no moral significance. Thus science was free to
exploit nature and to do so without any moral
inhibitions.

One result of the separation of man from nature
was the emergence of the concept of the world in
which there existed human consciousness on the
one hand and matter on the other. That is why, for
example, Descartes affirmed that because animals
have no soul, they neither think nor feel.

The establishment of science as the sovereign

form of human reason inevitably resulted in the humiliation of all other forms of human knowledge – moral, religious and traditional. They become marginalized within cultural life. As science was divided from morality, it could progress on its own without restraint. So it travelled independently from society in the confirmed belief that it had the right, and the duty, to investigate, discover and innovate.

These ideas are still at the very centre of our society. Recently, I received a pamphlet published in the important series called 'Contemporary Papers'. In it, the respected scientist Lewis Wolpert, Professor of Biology as Applied to Medicine in the Department of Anatomy and Development Biology at University College, London, explains the merits of science. Professor Wolpert is a Fellow of the Royal Society and Chairman of the Committee for the Public Understanding of Science.

He makes many interesting points. When discussing traditional farmers he says, 'They relied on experience and learned from their mistakes . . . It was an acquired skill based on learning and is, unlike science, closely linked to common sense . . . There is no reason to distinguish such inventiveness from an extension of the chimpanzees' ability to use tools.'

Discussing architecture, he writes: 'The great buildings of the Renaissance were not built on scientific principles, but practical experience. They relied on the five-minute theorem: if, when the props were removed, the building stood for five minutes, it was assumed it would stand for ever.'

Turning to agriculture, Professor Wolpert writes: 'If we accept battery hens . . . would we accept animals who had been engineered not to experience discomfort? At first sight this may not be acceptable, but it requires analysis of our attitudes towards farm animals rather than instant rejection. And we still have to think hard why introducing, for example, a gene from a fish into a tomato to keep it fresh longer seems, at first sight, unattractive. These are personal, almost aesthetic judgements . . .' Professor Wolpert then comments: 'We seem to have a desperate fear . . . of mixing together different sorts of organisms.' In another important point, he describes what he calls the technological imperative: 'If an experiment can be done, it will be done; if the knowledge is available, it will be applied.' Finally Professor Wolpert asserts: 'Whatever new technology is introduced, it is not for the scientists to make the moral or ethical decisions.'[4]

This pamphlet is an excellent demonstration of

Enlightenment thinking: the contempt in which science holds traditional farmers and architects; the idea that animals should be engineered to feel no pain, which is a development of the views of Descartes and of his disciple Malebranche, who described animals as unfeeling machines; the adoration of science; and a reaffirmation of Bacon's belief that scientific facts have no moral significance. The certainty of man's superiority over nature is well expressed when Professor Wolpert wonders why we could fear 'mixing together different sorts of organisms' by genetic engineering. Nature also rejects 'mixing'. Animals that are too distant genetically one from the other cannot interbreed. Different animals that are much closer, such as the horse and the donkey or the lion and the tiger, can interbreed but their offspring – mules, tigons and ligers – are sterile. Science rejects evolution as being too slow. It wants instantaneous transformation. It considers itself above nature, so why should it take any notice of its rules?

Modernists do not accept that each generation has a duty to commit to a contract between the past, the present and the future. They do not see themselves as guardians of continuity but rather as agents of constantly accelerating change. And they think only fleetingly of its potential consequences.

THE TRAP

The Enlightenment also believed in a universal civilization.

Yes, in addition to its belief in the transcendent supremacy of mankind and of reason, a universal civilization is the third component of the Enlightenment world view. This rests on the belief that cultural diversity is no more than an ephemeral phenomenon which occurs during our evolution towards universal humanity. Cultural differences, it was thought, would become minor residual elements in a cosmopolitan civilization, rather like ethnic cuisines in modern western cities. Universal civilization implies that the multitude of different cultures are no more than rivulets, whose fate is to flow into the great ocean of a cosmopolitan world-society.

Do you think that this belief still persists?

It does. Cultural imperialism is still very much alive. GATT and Somalia are among the multitude of current examples. Cultural imperialism is more deeply harmful than territorial expansion. The conquistadores in Latin America plundered, raped and usually returned home. They caused horrible injury. Their successors, the proselytizers, were responsible for the ultimate form of plundering.

They robbed whole nations of their language, identity and religion.

Enlightenment liberals today believe that if the world consists exclusively of democratic states there will be no war. Therefore, the corollary must also be true: radically different regimes cannot coexist in harmony. That is how Enlightenment thinkers have concluded that worldwide cultural homogenization is a precondition of peace. It follows that any community which resists the absorption or destruction of its culture by the West is a threat to peace.

What were the principal accomplishments of the Enlightenment? And what are its failings?

Its principal accomplishment has been the growth of scientific knowledge with the consequent development of modern technology. Its error was the elevation of reason, as embodied in science, technology and production, into an end in itself. It converted tools that were meant to serve the fundamental needs of society into demi-gods to be worshipped for their own sake. It produced extraordinary material innovation and economic growth. But it destroyed the diversity of cultures in which human beings have traditionally lived and in which their lives have found meaning. Progress and growth became surrogates for stability and contentment, which were considered to be encumbrances inhibiting the free development of human creativity.

Do you reject the achievements of the Enlightenment?

I reject its priorities. Not all its products.

Should the pursuit of science be constrained?

Obviously, scientific experimentation must be carried out in accordance with society's view of ethical behaviour. Science must not travel independently from the social needs of communities. Science does not have great wisdom. Rather it accumulates and cleverly analyzes particular information which supplies it with skills. It does not have an overall view based on general understanding. Science is massively powerful, potentially useful and, of course, can be beneficial. But as it solves problems, so it creates others. Scientific achievement produces both expected and unexpected results and the latter, quite often, can do more damage in the long term than the former do good.

Contrary to the views of Descartes, science should not be separated from the ethical or the spiritual; contrary to the views of Bacon, scientific facts do have a moral significance. Science must serve society and be a part of it. It is a tool and must be used with wisdom so as to improve the stability, contentment and sustainable prosperity of societies throughout the world.

What about technology, industry and the economy? How should we use them?

They are all useful instruments. But if uncontrolled by more fundamental values, they can destroy social stability and ultimately devour our civilization. During our conversations, I have attempted to describe two practical examples of technology running amok: nuclear energy and intensive agriculture. I also attempted to provide examples of what I believe to be beneficial and sustainable alternatives.

In any case, technology, industry, the economy and science must all serve the true needs of society. Stability and contentment should not be sacrificed so as to further the development of our tools.

You believe in free enterprise.

Yes. Of course, its forms will vary from culture to culture and must always be subject to their different traditions. But it can be a satisfactory system for our western societies. A free economy was the antidote to socialist and communist centralism. It represents more than just an effective economic system. It is a commitment to a certain type of society. It should be based on the limitation of the power of the state; supremacy of the law; economic and social decentralization; and free internal markets. Free enterprise functions best when families and citizens are self-reliant and retain responsibility for their own lives. It should be the antithesis of the centralized state which breeds a culture of dependency, destroys the will of the people and debilitates the nation. That is the moral and practical justification of free enterprise.

But the world has changed. Marxist centralism has been discredited. Societies have lifted their attention from the Cold War and are being forced to face different threats. Václav Havel wrote:

The fall of communism can be regarded as a sign that modern thought . . . has come to a final crisis. This era has created the first global, or planetary, technical civilization, but it has reached the limit of its potential, the point beyond which the abyss begins . . . Man's attitude to the world must be radically changed. We have to abandon the arrogant belief that the world is merely a puzzle to be solved, a machine with instructions for use waiting to be discovered, a body of information to be fed into a computer in the hope that sooner or later it will spit out a universal solution . . .[5]

Those of us who believe in free enterprise must understand that although in many nations and in many ways our beliefs remain eminently valid, on their own they are not sufficient. They must be integrated into the overriding imperatives of the biosphere as well as of human societies. Market forces must be harnessed to the needs of stable communities. Otherwise, like Marxists, we will be rejected as mechanistic relics of the past.

Earlier you said that science and technology were travelling independently without constraints. What do you propose?

That is the truly fundamental question. How do you discipline these modern demi-gods? It is only possible if we accept that they are subordinated to something greater than themselves. Saint Thomas Aquinas taught that the rational must be subordinated to the spiritual. Others, according to their religious traditions, use different words such as 'sacred' or 'the needs of society' or 'respect for nature'. We must each find our own definition. But all human societies need a spiritual engagement; without one, they are no more than counting machines.

To better understand the perplexity of modern western man, we must refer to the story of Genesis. 'So God created man in His own image . . . and God said: "Be fruitful and multiply and replenish the earth and subdue it; and have dominion over the fish of the sea, and over the fowl of the air, and over every living thing that moveth upon the earth." '[6]

Some concerned Christian theologians are reassessing their interpretation of these words. They consider that dominion does not equate with domination and that as the Bible also requires man to 'cultivate and take care of'[7] the earth, man has in fact been entrusted with the duty of stewardship of nature. This school of Christian thought is further comforted by the story of Noah's Ark, in which Noah is ordered by God to save two of every living species. This is interpreted as God's wish that we respect and protect diversity.

God's covenant was made with 'every living creature',[8] confirming the sacredness of all life, not just human life. In the Book of Genesis it is also said that God, after creating the earth, declared it 'very good'.[9]

These interpretations recreate a unity between science and the sacred. The earth is 'very good', so how can a Christian allow it to be ravaged? Man is the steward and as such has a responsibility for nature. Therefore, instead of travelling unrestrained, man's science must be sensitive to moral, ethical and social requirements.

The Christian philosopher Dr René Dubos said: 'We must take to heart the Biblical teaching: the Lord God took man and put him in the Garden of Eden to dress and to tend it. This means not only that the earth has been given to us for our enjoyment, but also that it has been entrusted to our care. Technologized societies thus far have exploited the earth: we must reverse this trend and learn to take care of it with love.'[10]

Welcome as this is, some believe that there is still further to go. In these interpretations, man, the steward, remains apart from nature and transcends all other living things. He and he alone is created in the 'image of God'. One of the most promising strands of Judeo-Christian thought was that of Saint Francis of Assisi, who considered all nature, not merely man, as the mirror of God and called all creatures his 'brothers' and 'sisters'. In the *Canticle of the Creatures* he speaks of 'brother' sun, wind and fire, 'sister' moon and water, and 'mother' earth. But his views were quickly forgotten, even by the Franciscan movement itself, because at the time the Church was struggling to suppress the indigenous European religions which believed in man's duty to revere nature.

What about God's command to 'be fruitful and multiply and replenish the earth'?

In *Life on Earth*, David Attenborough plots the history of life on the timescale of one year.[11] Based on that scale, if evolution started on 1 January, humans did not appear on earth until 31 December. For almost all of its life, the earth has existed without humanity. During the 1800 years from AD 1 to the birth of the Industrial Revolution it is estimated that human population grew from 250 million to 900 million. Then from 1800 to 1992, it grew to 5.5 billion. And by the year 2050, we are told, on present trends it will have grown to 9.6 billion.[12] Significantly, other living species have become extinct at a rate which follows the growth of human population.

What is more, we have compounded the problem by uprooting the populations of the world. Instead of encouraging family units rooted in their own stable communities, bound together by ancestral cultures and confident in their traditions, we have destroyed, and continue to do so, families, communities, cultures and traditions. Thus, not only have populations exploded in size, they have also become deracinated and desocialized.

Will man, in his perceived role of steward responsible for nature, succeed in achieving a level of human population compatible with his responsibility – in other words, a level which allows the natural environment to survive? Or will man fail and leave it to nature to restore an appropriate balance, as she has done so often in the past when population booms have been followed by population crashes?

How do these ideas, expressed in the story of Genesis, contrast with the beliefs of other great religions?

The ancient Chinese regarded man as having been created out of the fleas on the body of P'an Ku, the primal being by whose death and dismemberment the world was made. As Arthur Cotterell and Yong Yap comment: 'What stands out most for a Westerner is the lowly position the Chinese have ascribed to man; not the centre of creation, nor the colossus in the landscape, but rather a small figure in the great sweep of natural things.'[13]

In Buddhism and Hinduism, there is no deep gulf between the human species and other living creatures. All are subject to the same laws and to the same ultimate destiny. A striking example of the lack of anthropocentrism in Buddhist mythology is described in the book by Alexandra David-Neel, *Buddhism: Its Doctrines and Methods.*

A young prince, said to be the historical Buddha in one of his previous existences, is travelling through a forest. An abnormal drought has dried up the springs; the riverbeds are nothing but sand and stones; the leaves, calcined by a blazing sun, fall into dust, and the animals have fled elsewhere. There, in the midst of this desolation, the prince sees, close to him, in a thicket, a famished and dying tigress surrounded by her young. The beast sees him too, and her eyes blaze with ardent longing to launch herself upon this prey, so close to her, and to feed her young that she can no longer suckle, and who like her will die of starvation. But she lacks the strength to rise and leap at him . . . she remains outstretched, pitiable in her maternal distress and her longing for life.

Then the young prince, with perfect composure, turns aside from his path, and approaching the tigress, who could not reach him, he gives himself to her as food.[14]

The significance of this story is how different it is from most western legends. This is no happy ending. The prince is not saved at the last moment and for us, within the western tradition, his sacrifice is not credible.

In Japanese Shinto, the western distinction between the natural and the supernatural realms is altogether lacking. Nature itself is regarded as the site of the gods, the place of divinity. In Taoism, China's indigenous religion, man is not elevated above other species. Harmony with natural processes is man's proper relationship with the world, not the imposition of human will upon it.

What about the religious beliefs of primal peoples?

Perhaps the best way to illustrate the difference in viewpoints is to quote extracts from a letter attributed (whether rightly or wrongly is of no importance) to the American Indian chief Seattle, chief of the Dwamish, Suquamish and allied Indian tribes.[15] The letter, apparently written with the help of an amanuensis, is believed to have been sent in 1854 to President Franklin Pierce, following the request by the US government to acquire their tribal lands.

How can you buy or sell the sky, the warmth of the land? The idea is strange to us. If we do not own the freshness of the air and the sparkle of the water, how can you buy them? Every part of this earth is sacred to my people.

Every shining pine needle, every sandy shore, every mist in the dark woods, every clearing and humming insect is holy in the memory and experience of my people. The sap which courses through the trees carries the memories of the red man.

The white man's dead forget the country of their birth when they go to walk among the stars. Our dead never forget this beautiful earth, for it is the mother of the red man.

We are part of the earth and it is part of us. The perfumed flowers are our sisters; the deer, the horse, the great eagle, these are our brothers. The rocky crests, the juices in the meadows, the body heat of the pony, and man – all belong to the same family . . .

This shining water that moves in the streams and rivers is not just water but the blood of our ancestors . . . The rivers are our brothers, they quench our thirst . . .

We know that the white man does not understand our ways. One portion of land is the same to him as the next, for he is a stranger who comes in the night and takes from the land whatever he needs. The earth is not his brother but his enemy, and when he has conquered it, he moves on. He leaves his father's graves behind, and he does not care . . .

His father's grave and his children's birthright, are forgotten. He treats his mother, the earth, and his brother, the sky, as things to be bought, plundered, sold like sheep or bright beads. His appetite will devour the earth and leave behind only a desert . . .

What is man without the beasts? If all the beasts were gone, man would die from a great loneliness of spirit. For whatever happens to the beasts, soon happens to man. All things are connected . . .

Whatever befalls the earth befalls the sons of the earth . . . Man did not weave the web of life: he is merely a strand in it. Whatever he does to the web, he does to himself.

Notes

CHAPTER ONE

1. *National Income and Product Accounts of the United States: Vol. I, 1929–1958*, Washington: Government Printing Office, 1992; News release from the US Department of Commerce, Washington, 29 September 1994. US GNP figures are in 1987 prices.

2. Central Statistical Office, *UK National Accounts: 1994 Edition*, London: HMSO, 1994. UK GNP figures are in 1990 prices.

3. 'What About "Putting People First"?', *Los Angeles Times*, 8 September 1993.

4. Godson, R., and Olson, W., *International Organized Crime: Emerging Threat to US Security*, Washington: National Strategy Information Center, August 1993.

5. 'A Murder Shows the Crushing Cost of US Crime', *Washington Post*, 6 July 1994.

6. 'Les "Lendemains Qui Chantent" du Libre-Echangisme Mondiale', *Le Figaro*, Paris, 29 November 1993.

7. Institut National de la Statistique et des Etudes Economiques (INSEE), Paris, figures published on 7 March 1971 and 31 May 1994 respectively. (Among the groups excluded from the official French unemployment figures are, *inter alia*: all unemployed people over 57 years of age, the homeless, the long-term unemployed, and those

on various training programmes. Details are available from INSEE.)

8. Central Statistical Office, UK GNP figures at 1990 prices, 13 September 1994; Goodman, A., and Webb, S., *For Richer for Poorer: The Changing Distribution of Income in the United Kingdom, 1961–1991*, Commentary, No. 42, London: Institute for Fiscal Studies, June 1994. This study adopts the government's definition of people in poverty as those with incomes less than 50% of the mean income before housing costs.

9. King of Bhutan's annual speech, 1991.

CHAPTER TWO

1. Ricardo, D., *On the Principles of Political Economy and Taxation*, London: J. M. Dent and Sons, 1992.

2. World Bank, *World Population Projections: 1994–95 Edition*, Baltimore: Johns Hopkins University Press for The World Bank, August 1994.

3. In Borotra, F., *Rapport de la commission d'enquête de l'Assemblée nationale sur les délocalisations à l'étranger d'activités économiques*, Paris: Journal Officiel, 2 December 1993.

4. 'IBM is Overhauling Disk Drive Business, Cutting Jobs, Shifting Production to Asia', *Wall Street Journal*, New York, 5 August 1994.

5. 'Boeing to Expand China Operations, Names New Pres-

ident for Unit There', *Wall Street Journal*, New York, 9 August 1994.

6. 'US Multinationals take "Brain Work" to Plants Overseas', *Wall Street Journal Europe*, 30 September 1994.

7. 'Le TGV Seoul Pusan', *Le Figaro*, Paris, 19 April 1994; 'Industrie choisie de préférence à son concurrent Allemand, GEC Alsthom construira le TGV en Corée du Sud', *Le Monde*, Paris, 19 April 1994.

8. 'Industrie: Selon Henri Martre, président du GIFAS, la reprise dans l'aéronautique n'aura pas lieu avant 1995', *Le Monde*, Paris, 29 April 1993.

9. Goldin, I. and van der Mensbrugghe, D., *Trade Liberalization: What's at Stake*, Washington: World Bank and OECD, 1993.

10. 'Where Gatt's $200bn Really Comes From', *Financial Times*, London, 4 October 1993.

11. US Department of Labor Bureau of Labor Statistics, *Business Establishment Survey*, average hourly and weekly earnings of production or non-supervisory workers in 1982 dollars, provided from on-line search, 12 August 1994.

12. 'Elite companies rule world of trade', *Guardian*, London, 31 August 1994.

13. Daly, H., and Goodland, R., *An Ecological-Economic Assessment of Deregulation of International Commerce under GATT*, Washington: World Bank, September 1992.

14. Interview on French television channel TFI, 11 June 1994, and personal communication.

15. Dyos, H., and Wolff, M., *The Victorian City*, London: Routledge, 1973.

16. Department of Employment, *Employment Gazette*, London, September 1994.

17. Government Statistical Service, *Households Below Average Income*, London: HMSO, 1994.

18. 'Financial Indicators', *The Economist*, London, 5 November 1994.

19. 'Paying for the Foreign Debts', *Washington Post*, Final Edition, 3 November 1994.

CHAPTER THREE

1. 'Somalia Slips Back to Bloodshed', *Washington Post*, 4 September 1994.

2. 'Imposing Democracy: Could US Stop with Haiti?', *International Herald Tribune*, Paris, 10 September 1994.

3. The League of Nations took this action following the work of the International Commission of Inquiry to Investigate Slavery and Forced Labour in Liberia, chaired by Dr Cuthbert Christy.

4. *Encyclopaedia Britannica*, Chicago: Encyclopaedia Britannica, Vol. 12, 1994.

5. US Department of Justice, *Statistical Yearbook of the Immigration and Naturalization Service*, Washington: Government Printing Office, 1992, p. 29.

6. *Ibid.*, pp. 16, 30.

7. Reagan, R., in *Public Papers of the Presidents of the United States*, Washington: Government Printing Office, 1982. (The text is taken from the President's 'Remarks to the

People of Foreign Nations on New Year's Day', 1 January 1982.)

8. 'Beyond the Melting Pot', *Time*, 9 April 1990.

9. US Department of Justice, *op cit.*, pp. 27, 115.

10. Oakeshott, M., *Rationalism in Politics and Other Essays*, Minneapolis: Liberty Press, 1991.

11. Santayana, G., *Dominations and Powers: Reflections on Liberty, Society and Government*, New York: Charles Scribner's Sons, 1951.

12. Orwell, G., *The Collected Essays, Journalism, and Letters, Vol 2: My Country Right or Left, 1940–1943*, London: Penguin, 1970, p. 168. Orwell writes: 'The energy that actually shapes the world springs from emotions – racial pride, leader-worship, religious belief, love of war – which liberal intellectuals mechanically write off as anachronisms, and which they have usually destroyed so completely in themselves as to have lost all power of action.'

13. 'Europe: le réquisitoire de Claude Cheysson', *Le Figaro*, Paris, 7 May 1994.

14. 'EU Ministers tell court to uphold council secrecy', *Guardian*, London, 31 August 1994.

15. Speech by Jacques Delors to the European Parliament, 6 July 1988.

16. James Buchanan speaking in Paris, at a conference on constitutional issues, 1989.

17. CDU/CSU, *Reflections on European Policy*, published by the CDU/CSU Parliamentary Group in the German Bundestag, September 1994.

CHAPTER FOUR

1. 'The Moral Origins of the Urban Crisis' *Wall Street Journal*, New York, 8 May 1992.

CHAPTER FIVE

1. Personal communication from José Lutzenberger, September 1992.
2. Daly, H., and Cobb, J., *For the Common Good*, London: Green Print, 1991.
3. *World Urbanization Prospects: The 1992 Revision*, New York: United Nations, 1993.
4. Lacey, R., *Unfit for Human Consumption*, London: Souvenir Press, 1991, p. 32.
5. Crawford, M., Gale, M., Woodford, M. and Casperd, N., 'Comparative Studies on Fatty Acid Composition of Wild and Domestic Meats', *International Journal of Biochemistry*, New York, 1970, pp. 295–305; Crawford, M., 'Fat Animals – Fat People', *World Health*, Rome: World Health Organization, July–August 1991; Crawford, M. and Marsh, D., *The Driving Force, Food Evolution and the Future*, London: Heinemann, 1989, p. 228.
6. Food and Agriculture Organization and World Health Organization, *The Role of Dietary Fats and Oils in Human Nutrition*, Rome: Food and Agriculture Organization, 1978; Moncada, S. and Vane, J., 'Prostacyclin, Thro-

maoxane and Leukotrienes', *British Medical Bulletin*, 39, 1983, p. 209; World Health Organization, *Diet, Nutrition and the Prevention of Chronic Diseases*, Rome, 1990.

7. Crawford, M., Gale, M. and Woodford, M., 'Muscle and Adipose Tissue Lipids of the Warthog (Phacochoerus Aethiopicus)', *International Journal of Biochemistry*, New York, 1970, pp. 654–58; Crawford, M., Doyle, W., Drury, P., Ghebremskel, K., Harbige, L., Leyton, J. and Williams, G., 'The Food Chain for n-6 and n-3 Fatty Acids with Special Reference to Animal Products', in *Dietary w3 and w6 Fatty Acids: Biological Effects and Nutritional Essentiality*, London: Plenum Press, 1989, pp. 407–14.

8. Lacey, R., *op. cit.*, pp. 38–40.

9. Fraser, H., Farquhar, C., McConnell, I. and Davies, D., 'The Scrapie Disease Process is Unaffected by Ionizing Radiation', *International Journal of Biochemistry*, 317, New York, 1989, pp. 653–58; Gajdusek, D., 'Unconventional viruses and the origin and disappearance of Kuru', *Science*, 197, Washington, 1977, pp. 943–60; Brown, P., Liberski, P., Wolff, A. and Gajdusek, D., 'Resistance of Scrapie Infectivity to Steam Autoclaving after Formaldehyde Fixation and Limited Survival after Ashing at 360°: Practical and Theoretical Implications', *Journal of Infectious Diseases*, 115, Chicago, 1990, pp. 393–99.

10. Brown, P. and Gajdusek, D., 'Survival of the Scrapie Virus after 3 Years' Interment', *The Lancet*, 337, London, 1991, pp. 269–70.

11. Dealler, S., 'Bovine Spongiform Encephalopathy (BSE): The potential effect of the epidemic on the human

population', *British Food Journal*, 95, York, 1993, pp. 22–34.

12. *The Bovine Offal Prohibition Regulation*, London: HMSO, Statutory Instrument, No. 2061, 1989.

13. Lacey, R., *Mad Cow Disease*, St. Helier: Cypsela Publications (in press).

14. Southwood, R., *Report of the Working Party on Bovine Spongiform Encephalopathy*, London: HMSO, 1989.

15. 'EU backs Britain in row with Germany over BSE', *Independent*, London, 31 March 1994.

16. Dealler, S., *op. cit.*

17. Patterson, W. and Dealler, S., 'BSE and possible risk to human health: food for thought', *Journal of Public Health Medicine*, (accepted for publication).

18. Lacey, R., 'The BSE Epidemic', *Journal of Nutritional Medicine*, 3, Oxford, 1992, pp. 149–51.

19. 'Women's illness fans beef fears', *Guardian*, London, 28 January 1994.

20. Quoted in 'Mad Cows and Englishmen', *Independent*, London, 31 March 1994.

21. See for example the responses to the public consultation on BST held by the Veterinary Medicines Directorate of the Ministry of Agriculture, Fisheries and Food. The findings of this consultation, conducted in the summer of 1994, are available from the Ministry in London.

22. John Gummer at the Grassland South West Show, quoted in *Independent on Sunday*, London, 29 June 1991.

23. Leaked confidential Monsanto file, 'Toxicity of CP11

5099 in a Prolonged Release System in Lactating Cows',
13 January 1987, p. 28.

24. Letter from Congressman John Conyers, Chairman of the
Congressional Committee on Government Operations,
to the Hon. Richard P. Kusserow, Inspector General, US
Department of Health and Human Services, 8 May 1990.

25. Instructions for use of POSILAC, Animal Sciences Division of Monsanto Company, St Louis, April 1993.

26. 'Democrats' New Overseer Is Everybody's Mr Inside',
New York Times, 19 August 1994.

27. Quoted in 'The Milking of the Cash Cow', *Independent*,
London, 29 January 1994.

28. *Ibid.*

29. *Ibid.*

30. Fowler, C., Lachkovics, E., Mooney, P. and Shand, H.,
'The Laws of Life. Another Development and the New
Biotechnologies', *Development Dialogue*, 1–2, Sweden,
1988.

31. *Ibid.*

32. Fowler, C. and Mooney, P., *The Threatened Gene*, Cambridge: Lutterworth Press, 1991, pp. 58, 60.

33. *Ibid.*, p. 143.

34. Hindmarsh, R., 'The Flawed "Sustainable" Promise of
Genetic Engineering', *The Ecologist*, Sturminster
Newton, September 1991, pp. 198–99.

35. Burch, D., Hulsman, K., Hindmarsh, R. and Brownlea,
A., 'Biotechnology Policy and Industry Regulation: Some
Ecological, Social and Legal Considerations', submission
to the House of Representatives Standing Committee on

Industry, Science and Technology Inquiry into Genetically Modified Organisms, Australia, September 1990.

36. 'Healthy Crops – Simply Irresistible', *Economist*,
London, 10 August 1991.

37. Fowler, C. and Mooney, P., *op. cit.*, p. 43.

38. *Ibid*, p. x.

39. *Ibid*, p. x.

40. Pimentel, D., 'Environmental and Economic Benefits of
Sustainable Agriculture', in Paoletti, M., Napier, T.,
Ferro, O., Stinner, B. and Stinner, D., eds., *Socio-Econ-
omic and Policy Issues for Sustainable Farming Systems*,
Padua: Cooperativa Amicizia, 1993, pp. 5–20.

CHAPTER SIX

1. Statement by Lewis Strauss, Chairman of the US Atomic
Energy Commission, to the National Association of
Science Writers in New York, 16 September 1954.

2. Rand, M., *Energy Research and Development: A Story of
Misplaced Priorities*, Energy Series No. 5, London:
Greenpeace International, March 1992.

3. United States Department of Energy, *Annual Energy
Review 1991*, Washington: Government Printing Office,
1991.

4. Spencer, D., 'A Preliminary Assessment of Carbon Diox-
ide Mitigation Options', *Annual Review of Energy and
Environment*, 16:264, Snowmass, Colorado: Rocky
Mountain Institute, 1991.

5. Piette, M–A., Krause, F. and Verderber, R., *Technology Assessment: Energy-Efficient Commercial Lighting*, Lawrence Berkeley Laboratory, LBL-27032, 1989, and communications from John Hoffman, Director, Global Change Unit, US Environmental Protection Agency to Rocky Mountain Institute.

6. *Technology Atlas: Lighting* (1988, 1994); *Drivepower* (1989, 1993); *Appliances* (1990); *Water Heating* (1991); *Space Cooling and Air Handling* (1992), *Space Heating* (1993); all from E SOURCE (Boulder, Colorado 80302–5114, USA), which updates the information with bi-monthly supplements.

7. *Ibid.*; Lovins, A. and Lovins, H., 'Least-Cost Climatic Stabilization', in *Annual Review of Energy and Environment*, Snowmass, Colorado: Rocky Mountain Institute, 1991.

8. *Technology Atlas, op. cit.*

9. Fickett, A., Gellings, C. and Lovins, A., 'Efficient Use of Electricity', *Scientific American*, New York, September 1990, pp. 64–74.

10. Sweden: Krause, F., Bach, W. and Koomey, J., *Energy Policy in the Greenhouse*, Vol. 1, El Cerrito, California: International Project for Sustainable Energy Paths, 1989; Krause, F., Koomey, J., Olivier, D. and Radanne, P., *The Cost of Carbon Reductions: A Case Study of Western Europe*, Vol. 2, El Cerrito, California: International Project for Sustainable Energy Paths, 1993; Bodlund, B. et al., 'The Challenge of Choices: Technology Options for the Swedish Electricity Sector', in Johannson, T., Bod-

JAMES GOLDSMITH

lund B. and Williams, R., eds., *Electricity*, Lund University Press, 1989, pp. 883–947; see also Johansson, T. and Steen, P., *I Stället för Kärnkraft: Energi År 2000*, Stockholm: Industridepartementet, DsI 18, 1983. Denmark: Nørgård, J., 'Low Electricity Appliances – Options for the Future', in Johansson, T., Bodlund B. and Williams, R., *Electricity*, Lund University Press, 1989, pp. 125–72. Germany: Feist, W., *Electricity Saving Potential in Private Households in The Federal Republic of Germany*, Darmstadt: Institute of Housing and the Environment, 1987.

11. Lovins, A., Barnett, J. and Lovins, L., 'Supercars: The Coming Light Vehicle Revolution', paper presented at the European Council for an Energy Efficient Economy, Rungstedgärd, Denmark, 4 June 1993; Lovins, A. and Lovins, H., 'Reinventing the Wheels', *Atlantic Monthly*, New York, in press for January 1995.

12. Hamrin, J. and Rader, N., *Investing in the Future: A Regulator's Guide to Renewables*, Washington: National Association of Regulatory Utility Commissioners, 1993; Personal communication from Karen Griffin, California Energy Commission, to WorldWatch Institute, 26 April 1994.

13. United States Department of Energy, *Annual Energy Review 1991*, Washington: Government Printing Office, 1991.

14. DiPippo, R., 'Geothermal Energy', *Energy Policy*, Oxford, October 1991.

15. Department of Energy, *US Geothermal Energy R&D*

210

Program Multi-Year Plan, 1988–1992, Washington: Government Printing Office, 1992.

16. Hock, S., Thresher, R. and Williams, T., 'The Future of Utility-Scale Wind Power', in Burley, S. and Arden, M., eds., *Advances in Solar Energy: An Annual Review of Research and Development*, Boulder, Colorado: American Solar Energy Society, 1992.

17. Grubb, M. and Meyer, N., 'Wind Energy: Resources, Systems and Regional Strategies', in Johannson, T. et al., eds., *Renewable Energy: Sources for Fuels and Electricity*, Washington: Island Press, 1993.

18. De Laquil III, P. et al., 'Solar-Thermal Electric Technology', in Johansson, T. et al., eds., *Renewable Energy: Sources for Fuels and Electricity*, Washington: Island Press, 1993.

19. Solar Energy Research Institute, *The Potential for Renewable Energy*, Golden, Colorado: National Renewable Energy Laboratory, Interlaboratory White Paper, SER/TP–260–3674, March 1990.

20. 'Cost of Closing Reactors Crucial to Privatisation', *Independent*, London, 5 July 1988.

21. House of Commons Energy Committee, *The Structure, Regulation and Economic Consequences of Electricity Supply in the Private Sector*, London: HMSO, 3rd Report, 1988.

22. *Hansard*, London: HMSO, 24 July 1989.

23. 'UK Electricity Privatisation: A Cabinet Document Leaks', *Power in Europe*, London, 31 October 1989.

24. Lawson, N., *The View from No. 11: Memoirs of a Tory Radical*, London: Bantam Press, 1992.

25. 'Nuclear Electric Hopes that No Nukes will be Good News', *Independent*, London, 27 July 1994.

26. National Audit Office, *The Cost of Decommissioning Nuclear Facilities*, London: HMSO, 27 May 1993.

27. British Nuclear Fuels Annual Report and Accounts, 1988; House of Commons Select Committee on Energy, *BNFL: reports and accounts*, London: HMSO, April 1989.

28. 'Nuclear site clean-up costs more than double to £8.2 bn', *Financial Times*, London, 18 June 1994.

29. Gilinsky, V. and Bupp, I., *Decision Brief: Premature Nuclear Plant Closings*, Cambridge, Massachusetts: Cambridge Energy Research Associates, November 1992.

30. Cour des Comptes, *Rapport au Président de la République*, Paris, Tome II, 1990, p. 210.

31. Presented by the VDEW (German Electricity Generators Association) and UNIPEDE (International Union of Producers and Distributors of Electrical Energy), at a press conference at the Hannover Exhibition, 21 April 1993.

32. *Nuclear Power Stations in the World 1994*, Paris: Atomic Energy Commission, 31 December 1993.

33. Ministère de l'Industrie, des Postes et Télécommunications et du Commerce Extérieur, *Les coûts de référence: Production électrique d'origine thermique*, Paris, 1993.

34. Electricité de France, 'Stratégie Commerciale d'EDF, 1990–1992', unpublished internal report.

35. In Yarochinskaya, A., *Tchernobyl, Vérité Interdite*, Paris: Editions de l'Aube, 1993.

36. *Ibid.*
37. The text of this speech can be found in the Deutscher Bundestag's *Stenographischer Bericht*, 220 Sitzung, Bonn, Friday, 6 June 1986.
38. 'Chernobyl Cost $55bn in Medical Aid', *East European Energy Report*, February 1993.
39. Yarochinskaya, *op. cit.*
40. *Ibid.*
41. 'Une soixantaine de victimes de Tchernobyl en grève de la faim à l'hôpital', *Enerpresse*, Paris, 28 April 1993.
42. 'Chernobyl caused 24-fold rise in thyroid cancer', Reuter, 23 April 1993.
43. Study by researchers from the University of Bern, reported on Greenbase by Agence France Presse, 17 September 1994.
44. 'Russia: forgotten victims of Chernobyl taking their own lives', IPS/*Moscow Times*, 12 January 1993.
45. Dumonceau, D., 'Conséquences de l'explosion nucléaire de Tchernobyl sur 'l'evolution des grossesses en Novège', *La Lettre du Gynécologue*, 152, Paris, October 1991.
46. 'Comment faire passer le nucléaire dans les moeurs?', *Enerpresse*, 24 May 1993.
47. Belbeoch, B. and Belbeoch, R., *Tchernobyl, Une Catastrophe*, Paris: Editions Allia, 1993, p. 187.
48. Hayes, R., Director General, British Nuclear Industry Forum, in a letter to *The Times*, London, 15 July 1994.
49. 'Chernobyl shield crumbling', *Independent*, London, 21 April 1994.

50. 'West funds reactors to replace Chernobyl', *New Scientist*, London, 16 July 1994.

51. *Ibid.*

52. 'US Ukraine Evaluation of Energy Options to Replace the Chernobyl Nuclear Plant', Department of Nuclear Energy in the Department of Energy, Washington, 23 June 1994.

53. 'Energy crisis blocks Chernobyl deal', *New Scientist*, London, 30 April 1994.

54. 'Nucléaire à l'Est . . . Un entretien avec Jean Syrota', *La Tribune Desfossés*, Paris, 25 April 1994.

55. 'Fatal blast at "retired" reactor', *New Scientist*, London, 23 April 1994.

56. Tanguy, P., *Rapport de synthèse: La sûreté nucléaire à EdF à fin 1989*, Paris: Inspection Générale pour la Sûreté Nucléaire, 8 January 1990.

57. Tanguy, P., *Sûreté Nucléaire 1993: rapport de l'Inspecteur général pour la sûreté nucléaire*, Paris: Electricité de France, 1994.

58. Schneider, M., et al., *Vessel Head Penetration Cracking in Nuclear Reactors*, Amsterdam: Greenpeace International, March 1993.

59. French Ministry of Industry bulletin, *Sûreté Nucléaire*, Paris, October 1993.

60. 'First circumferential penetration crack weld found at Ringhals–2', *Nucleonics Week*, New York, 10 June 1993.

61. *Ibid.*

62. On-line search of the French Ministry of Industry's Magnuc database, 28 September 1992.